And Shearer Has Won It!

by
J. Doyle

And Shearer Has Won It

First published in the United Kingdom by Club Books, 2014.

© Cover efks

Design by Plan4 Media

A catalogue record of this book is available from the British Library.   ISBN 978-1-907463-81-5

Contents

Introduction   7
Moneyless Chelsea   11
Triffic Decision   20
David Beckham: England Manager   33
The West Yorkshire Samba Beat   45
… and Shearer has won it   55
Turnip Taylor   66
The English Wizard   73
The Head of God   86
Akinbiyi, Goal Machine   96
Ray Wilkins, FIFA President   103
Bald Baggio   110
Seeing Red   121
Zizou   130
They Think It's All Over … It Is Now   139
Marching on Together   148
Argentine Dominance   158
Bloemfontein Ghost Goal   171
Bayern's Famous Treble   180
Aguer-d'oh   189
The New Galacitco   201
Ronald'oh!   212
Michael 'Sicknote' Owen   220
Scary and Becks   229

INTRODUCTION

Football is a sport that can divide opinion not only across the pubs and cafés up and down the country, but outside the stadium by the burger van or in terraces itself, or even from the comfort of your own home. What formation should the gaffer play? Why did he sell our star striker to Spain for lower than his asking price?

For instance, the world curled up in their beds, chipped away at their nails and parked the minimal amount of backside onto the edge of their seats and grew as one to will on Africa in the 2010 World Cup. A match in particular from that tournament was the Quarter-Final in Johannesburg between Uruguay and the sole African contender at that stage, Ghana (which I will talk about later, in much greater depth.)

The world stood, with baited breath as Asamoah Gyan distributed the ball into orbit in the last kick of extra time from the penalty spot. Of course, the combination of an audacious Sebastien Abreu chipped penalty which claimed Uruguay's semi-final spot and Luis Suarez's adequate impression of Diego Maradona to save a blatant goal for the Ghanaians left the South American nation as the pantomime villain, crushing not just the hopes of Africa with a single hand, but the hopes of every man, woman, child and possibly dog as the sentimental favourite to win the tournament in their home continent.

With these elements taken into account and from the sheer history of the sport, football is rapidly becoming not just a sport but for many fans a way of life – a religion if you will.

For a smattering of fans, the fans that are put through the excruciating penalty shootouts, the heartbreaking last minute defeats and the ecstasy of the trophies, it is indeed a matter of life and death – the importance is absolute.

Admittedly, football has been the diversion necessary for me to hurl myself through the first couple of decades in my life. From the lashing of a right foot, thirty yards from goal out on a patch of grass in Lens, France courtesy of David Beckham in a World Cup group stage game against Colombia I was hooked.

Growing up as a Manchester United fan in 1998, I endured one of the easiest births into the full-time role that is football supporter. Two Premier League titles off the back of a legendary treble-winning season wasn't bad going for the newly-knighted Sir Alex Ferguson and his latest Red Devils fan, me.

Football is important to me and, for those reading, I am certain that you are the ones that fill the away end, that travel through the thick fog and snow from the south just to see a deflated performance from your side and a battering on the north east coast – the passionate ones.

The miniscule occurrences, such as the flick of a Teddy Sheringham head or a subsequent prod into the net from a Norwegian talisman, the whole shape of footballing history can shift into a new parallel universe.

I am also certain that some readers know of *The Butterfly Effect*, a form of chaos theory and 2004 motion picture which depicted how changing a minute detail can catastrophically or, depending on your preference, fortunately subvert the history that we all know and might not necessarily cherish.

In … *And Shearer has won it*, I tell the tale of some previously unearthed football stories, chiefly because they haven't being allowed to happen due to a series of unfortunate (or fortunate) events.

These events document such unseen paradigms like Alan Shearer signing for Manchester United, instead of opting for a Keegan tirade-ridden tenure at Newcastle. What would the shape of football be like if Maradona rose above Peter Shilton and headed the ball in that 1986 World Cup quarter-final against England, or if Roy Keane was given a lifetime ban for his tackle on Alf-Inge Haaland? What if the Leeds United mass exodus of the early 21st century didn't happen?

Could you possibly imagine a world, not only just the footballing world, where Ryan Giggs chose to play for England as opposed to Wales? What if Roberto Baggio elected to have a short back and sides instead of that ponytail? Who would be best suited to become Sepp Blatter's inevitable successor as FIFA president? Would it be the *Addams Family* Uncle Fester look-a-like and *Sky Sports* pundit and former Manchester United and Chelsea player in Ray Wilkins?

Where would Chelsea be if they weren't purchased by Roman Abramovich, and Manchester United if they didn't win the 1999 UEFA Champions League final, for which this publication owes its name from the famous commentary from *ITV's* Clyde Tyldesley?

What if certain goals counted, others were disallowed and jobs of superb managers were kept or lost whilst shrewd and shocking appointments were made by the best names in the business?

David Beckham speaks not only for football but for charity and spreading football across the globe, but what if he plumped for Scary over Posh? What if he became England manager?

Figures of the great game – Lionel Messi, Eric Cantona, Sergio Aguero, Pele and Roy Keane, how could their careers be misshapen, diluted or contorted and pulled around?

It all lies within this collection of short football stories.

1
Moneyless Chelsea

The date was May the 11th, 2003 and the final day of the 2002-03 FA Premier League season. Liverpool travelled down the M1 to Stamford Bridge where they would ultimately have a play-off for the fourth and final UEFA Champions League berth for the upcoming 2003-04 season.

In reality, goals from Marcel Desailly and Jesper Gronkjaer sealed Chelsea's first Champions League place in four seasons. The match billed as the £20 million match, which resulting in Roman Abramovich's purchase of Chelsea and a return, for the first time in fifty years, to the glory days as Chelsea would win three league titles in 2005, 2006 and 2010 in Abramovich's sweeping domination of the English game.

Under Abramovich's ownership for the opening ten years, there was a high staff turnover, not just including the playing staff but also the management. The likes of Ranieri, Mourinho, Grant, Scolari to name a few came and went as Abramovich dealt with eight managers in nine seasons as well as spending almost seven hundred million pounds as the Hasselbainks, Flos and Zolas of this world transformed into the Torres', Drogbas and Essiens in a swift turnaround.

The turnaround for 'The Pensioners' was complete in May 2012 after they claimed the trophy which Abramovich craved as Chelsea defeated Bayern Munich in a penalty shootout in their own backyard in the UEFA Champions League final at the Allianz

Arena. It was all thanks to a twenty-four million portion of that seven hundred in Didier Drogba who signed off his Chelsea career in suitable fashion with a late equaliser and the winning penalty in the shootout.

Liverpool beat Chelsea 1-0 to win a spot in 2003-04's Champions League, with Roman Abramovich opting to purchase Liverpool.

Chelsea made no real signings in the summer but the crucial news coming out of Stamford Bridge remained the sale of Gianfranco Zola for nine million pounds to Lazio. Without Zola, the penetration is lacking from Chelsea and after consequently being fed into the UEFA Cup first round from their final day loss against Liverpool, they are pitted against Mallorca. Two stalemates occur both at the Bridge and in the return leg on the Balearic Island.

Chelsea shockingly crash out on penalties at the Iberostar Stadium as Eidur Gudjohnsen tamely strokes the ball into the welcoming arms of the Mallorca goalkeeper. Come October, Abramovich's investment of Liverpool looks a shrewd piece of football business as he swiftly shows Gerard Houiller the door following a brief pre-season under the French manager who had brought Liverpool four trophies just a mere two years previously.

The oil-rich Russian promptly welcomes Marcello Lippi, triggering a release clause of a million pounds from his Juventus contract, just a year prior to its expiration. Lippi brings in key names from Serie A such as the talismanic Ukrainian forward in Andriy Shevchenko as well as the experienced centre half in Paolo Maldini. They, alongside an increasingly unsettled Steven Gerrard provide the cornerstone to the Liverpool side who become Premier League champions for the first time in fourteen years.

In a pre-match build-up interview with *Football Focus*, Steven Gerrard highlights his unrest with Ray Stubbs prior to a contest in April 2004 at Highbury which was all important in preventing the unstoppable force that was the unbeaten Arsenal from winning the Premier League title.

Gerrard would later dismiss rumours of his departure to a floundering Chelsea by netting twice in a 3-1 win at Highbury which meant that the Anfield club would leapfrog Arsenal with just four matches remaining. The captain is punished for his interview just weeks prior to the final weekend of the league calendar and is astonishingly stripped of his captaincy going into the all-important final game of the season away at Southampton. The affectionately known, 'Stevie G' rattled in the winning goal at St. Mary's Stadium as Arsenal were held at Charlton Athletic which left Liverpool with a four-point lead, sealing their 19th top flight league title, improving upon their record of top flight titles won and keeping their distance from Sir Alex Ferguson's Manchester United who finished in fourth place for the first time in Premier League history, a record low.

Contrastingly, Chelsea loomed over the brink of financial trouble with boss Claudio Ranieri. As the end of the season approached, many pundits across the board believed that Chelsea were only spared their administration status by an appearance in the League Cup final where they were humiliated by an Arsenal side who ran out 5-0 winners in a crushing display from Thierry Henry, Robert Pires and Freddie Ljungberg. The Arsenal trio were soon snapped up by Liverpool for a total of fifty-three million pounds in a deal which would further unsettle Steven Gerrard, not only out of his captaincy but out of his beloved Anfield altogether.

Once Stevie was wrestled out of his captain's armband, he entered negotiations with a couple of months left on his contract with Chelsea manager, Claudio Ranieri who instigated a switch with Frank Lampard who was largely uninspiring in Chelsea's 11th place league finish in 2004.

Ranieri was ousted from his position at Stamford Bridge despite the incredible acquisition, and was replaced with Everton boss, David Moyes as the likes of Marcel Desailly and Eidur Gudjohnsen both aborted the sinking ship aboard Stamford Bridge.

Moyes, as well as bringing in Steven Gerrard, welcomed Tim Cahill after an impressive FA Cup final display against Manchester United where his Millwall side were beaten 3-0 at the Millennium Stadium in Cardiff. With the attraction of Frank Lampard and the almost-invincible talent shipped from North London, Ronaldinho admitted that he couldn't stay away from Anfield in an interview with *Sky Sports'* Jim White, signing from Barcelona a year into his contract for a whopping thirty-one million pounds – breaking Liverpool's transfer record for a single player.

The Liverpool side, who snatched the 'invincibles' tag from Arsenal a mere four matches from the end of the 2003-04 season, were seemingly becoming the untouchables of the division. Liverpool acted quick in snapping up John Terry who abandoned Chelsea for only seven million in the summer of 2004, in a season which saw Liverpool not only record their fifth Champions League trophy but achieve a successive Premier League title. Despite not being all that impressive in terms of goals, Lampard and Ronaldinho claimed the league title with five matches to spare, with Lippi exclaiming, a little bit worse for wear that he was 'The Special One, with the greatest club team of all-time' in a post-match interview with Geoff Shreeves when the title was won in a 4-0 win over Charlton Athletic at Anfield in April 2005.

Fast-forward almost three years to the exact date where Chelsea threw away their Champions League spot to Liverpool in 2003, Lippi and especially Frank Lampard were rueing their last day defeat to Chelsea who won their first league title for fifty-one years in 2006. Steven Gerrard was finding his feet without Lampard at Chelsea but the two were proving to become a dream come true in international football for England and manager Sven-Goran Eriksson.

Even the mere mention of the combination would begin the stirring in any Englishman's belly approaching the 2006 FIFA World Cup. Gerrard's double against Trinidad and Tobago in the group stages in Nurnberg got them through a tricky 3-0 win but otherwise England were unscathed as they marched through Sweden, Paraguay and Ecuador to reach Portugal in the quarter final stage in Gelsenkirchen.

Without the red carded Wayne Rooney an hour into the match, England filled the stadium with confidence as the contest spilled out onto a penalty shootout, despite their shootout loss to the Portuguese a mere two years prior in the European Championships.

This time, England shone as both Lampard and Gerrard converted their penalties with Jamie Carragher, Owen Hargreaves and Michael Owen all netting in a 5-3 shootout win. Despite the hopes of a nation resting on two midfielders' shoulders, the pair were undeterred going into the semi-final against hosts Germany and after Peter Crouch's late volley, England thought they were headed for a first World Cup final in forty years on from the success in their own backyard.

Ironically, it was the Germans again who stood in their way and with a late double through Lukas Podolski and Miroslav Klose, they ended all hopes of an English dream in the World Cup final in Berlin. The third place play-off though, of any World Cup, usually passes without incident with the world becoming no wiser for having viewed any of them.

However, the great English self-destruction in the contest against Italy has become an infamous story re-told down the years, leaving many supporter bemused after throwing away a two-goal lead to lose 4-2 to the Italians.

On any other occasion, in a play-off such as this, nobody would have cared should England have lost the match 4-2 without incident. The night belonged to the fight on 77 minutes between both Gerrard and Lampard, the supposed English dream midfield partnership. A two-goal lead had been surrendered by England and after Lampard overlooked a simple pass which would have seen the Chelsea midfielder, Steven Gerrard through on goal for a possible match winner, Gerrard went beserk and charged down the Liverpool playmaker.

Despite being on opposite ends of the field, Stevie G took it upon himself to run the width of the pitch, nibbling on Lampard's ear with complaints. The Liverpool captain didn't take kindly to the ringing in his ear and the old cliché of a push coming to a shove was happening right in front of Sven-Goran Eriksson's Swedish eyes on the touchline.

I am sure, that to this day, neither men are proud of what transpired in the next thirty seconds or so as Lampard flung a right hand into Gerrard's face which was returned with the agility of a professional boxer and the Liverpool man was left on the German turf with Gerrard towering over Frank, standing as though he was the victor in a heavyweight boxing contest.

The masses of teammates, opponents, officials and English coaching staff flooded the touchline where the madness had ensued only for Lampard to thrust himself with amazing strength, clattering Gerrard first with his head then with a series of punches that Mike Tyson would be proud of.

Steve McClaren had the daunting task of pulling Frank Lampard from the field of play which had becoming a momentary boxing ring, or dojo had the situation worsened. England were already resigned to defeat with two fewer men following both men's red cards and the Juventus forward, Alessandro del Piero would strike twice late on in the day as Italy ran out 4-2 winners, claiming third place.

McClaren, in a *FourFourTwo* interview in May 2011 shortly after a third Eredivisie title with PSV Eindhoven, stated that 'they [Gerrard and Lampard] were like savage animals,' recalling the incident in Stuttgart in July 2006, 'it took seven of us to prise them apart in the dressing room, they were rabid, almost foaming at the mouth.'

In his newly acquired accent, McClaren re-laid the story in both the tabloids and in his 2013 autobiography, *Double Dutch*. The consequences were rife for both Lampard and Gerrard who were suspended for nine months for their clubs which effectively meant a suspension from the 2006-07 season whilst a ban until the World Cup qualification campaign for the 2010 tournament in South Africa was put forward and passed by FIFA.

It seemed that, as neither men were getting younger, they were stuttering into their last legs of their careers. Chelsea dropped down the league ladder despite a miraculous previous season with Liverpool suffering, floundering to third position as they claimed their worst place in four seasons, since Abramovich's acquisition of the Anfield club.

Consequently, Lippi was out of a job and replaced with England manager candidate Sam Allardyce who immediately brought Carling Cup success in 2008 thanks to a late Frank Lampard goal, his first since the World Cup a mere two years previously.

In the meantime, without Gerrard, Chelsea achieved fourteenth position and were kept up with a 2-1 last day win over Fulham alongside a run of favourable results for David Moyes.

Steven Gerrard would leave Chelsea without playing another game, joining former manager Gerard Houiller at Manchester City for the 2007-08 season. Without their star player, Ken Bates put Chelsea on the market for Malcolm Glazer, who injected millions of debt into the Stamford Bridge club upon his purchase of the West London club.

A mere six seasons later, Steven Gerrard was picking up his fourth Premier League medal with Manchester City following their oil-rich owner's acquisition of the Eastlands club. Meanwhile, Frank Lampard was rotting on the substitutes bench at Tottenham Hotspur and Chelsea were, following two stints in administration, docked ten points for each and were finally relegated from the top flight in 2011 before dropping a further division in 2013 thanks to another points deduction, falling into League One, grouped with clubs of the calibre of Shrewsbury Town, Fleetwood Town and Bradford City.

2

Triffic Decision

Harry Redknapp has managed many a club and for his exploits in transforming a faltering Premier League team destined for relegation into an established figure at the top English table of football, he has earned the nickname 'Harry Houdini' with the press, unless you don't count that spell in the 2004-2005 season where he was unable to conjure up any magic on the south coast in Southampton, and the subsequent period in 2013 when his QPR side were relegated from the top flight.

After a long playing career at the likes of West Ham, Bournemouth and even a short stay across the Atlantic in Seattle, Redknapp was in the managerial hot seat, testing the waters at Bournemouth. The wheeler dealer, as he became better known, took charge of his old club, West Ham in 1994 with the sole aim to solidify their position in the Premier League.

No less than seven years later, Redknapp had built an empire on the East End of London, a footballing one, no less, he had crusaded around Europe with the Hammers, with his young band of academy graduates, figures like Rio Ferdinand, Frank Lampard, Joe Cole and Michael Carrick who have all won multiple Premier League titles, with Joe Cole the only one not to receive a UEFA Champions' League winners medal. Along with the maverick Paolo di Canio, Stuart Pearce and Trevor Sinclair also boosted their careers with the young starlets in the squad. Redknapp had blended a perfect mixture which landed West Ham the European dream – a cut-short holiday in the summer of 1999 as they prepared for the UEFA Intertoto Cup in July, wishing for a UEFA Cup berth which would become realised with a 3-1 away win in Metz. By November 1999, the Hammers were dumped out of Europe by Steaua Bucharest, 2-0 on aggregate and Redknapp would leave the following season.

'Arry graced the Director of Football's position at Portsmouth in 2001 before jumping back into the irresistible managerial hot seat at Fratton Park in March 2002. Just fourteen months later, Redknapp would exchange divisions as he gained automatic promotion to the Premier League, passing West Ham on the way up, who were subjected two years in the second tier of English football.

Meanwhile, on the south coast, Harry was living up to his billing, keeping Portsmouth in the division at the first time of asking but just six months after performing heroics, he resigned as the manager thanks to Portsmouth's infamous owner, Milan Mandaric who apparently had forced Redknapp out of the club.

Only a matter of weeks had passed before Redknapp jumped the south coast ship from Portsmouth to Southampton, leading to many upset Pompey fans to label him Judas. However, after sending the Saints down into the Championship, he was welcomed back with open arms at Fratton Park, staving off relegation for Portsmouth towards the back end of the 2005-06 season. Redknapp would improve upon his Houdini skills, lifting Pompey out of the bottom half of the table altogether, placing ninth in 2007, their best league position since 1955.

Portsmouth were riding high and improved further

on their league position, placing eighth but better was to follow. After beating Manchester United with both Bournemouth and West Ham, he managed to pip Sir Alex Ferguson's side to another FA Cup semi-final with a win at Old Trafford in March 2008 and Redknapp would lead Portsmouth into their first FA Cup final in sixty-nine years.

Nwankwo Kanu would be Pompey's hero in the final, scoring the winning goal against Cardiff City at Wembley and as a direct consequence, Portsmouth were in Europe. Portsmouth fans were fulfilling a lifetime's worth of ambitions through Harry Redknapp, the manager was soon receiving the freedom to the City of Portsmouth, with the ceremony untimely coming two days after his switch to White Hart Lane.

Just a month later, however, Portsmouth were leading A.C. Milan 2-0 on a soggy Thursday night at Fratton Park, only to have their dreams dashed by a late pair of goals by Filippo Inzaghi and Ronaldinho no less.

Harry Redknapp stays on as Portsmouth manager and second half goals from Younes Kaboul and Nwankwo Kanu seal a historic European night at Portsmouth as they defeat A.C. Milan 2-0.

In negotiations the next morning, Harry Redknapp persuades Jermain Defoe to stay at the club, whilst improving his wage and keeping him on at Fratton Park until 2011. The rejuvenation of Portsmouth is stuttered as they fail to defend their FA Cup crown at the first time of asking on an icy pitch in Blackpool, with Peter Crouch missing a penalty in a 3-1 shocking defeat in the third round of the tournament.

Crouch, who had lost his way through January would regain his form and the partnership up front with

Defoe through the latter months of the season with Crouch's six goals in four matches throughout March, which included a hat-trick against Everton at Fratton Park in a 5-1 demolition.

That crowning moment in March would destroy Everton's chances of European football as they were subsequently eliminated from the FA Cup in a semi-final with Manchester United in a penalty shootout. Everton would crumble in the league, finishing eighth, whilst Portsmouth would leapfrog them, reaching for bigger and better things.

Whilst Portsmouth would be eliminated at the round of sixteen stage in the UEFA Cup to an away goals defeat from Werder Bremen, it left Pompey to play up in only the Premier League. This suited Redknapp and his players down to the ground as they took 16 points from a possible final 21 points, narrowly missing out on the Champions League places to Arsenal, by just a few points, placing fifth.

Redknapp was the first to admit that his team wasn't ready to break the top four, but little did he know, that 12 months on, Redknapp would officially start the siege on the elite four of the Premier League. The foundations were set on the opening day of the season as Peter Crouch nicked the only goal of the game at Anfield on a sunny day in Liverpool, prompting jubilant scenes in the away end.

It was clear from the outset in the 2009-10 season that Redknapp was after silverware, not to further improve Portsmouth's league position. In a post-match interview in December 2009, after romping home to a 3-0 home win over Spartak Moscow in the re-branded Europa League, Redknapp reminded the audience that "the likes of Everton and Aston Villa had looked to plunder that fourth position but neither reaped the rewards, and neither shall we." This would be a preview of what was to come in the hotly anticipated League Cup semi-final ties across January with Southampton, who had bounced back from final day survival in May 2009 to hit their stride in the league and in the League Cup, with successive wins over Sunderland and Aston Villa away from home.

It would be the end of the road for Southampton though as Harry Redknapp was booed off the St. Mary's turf after a 2-0 second leg victory, claiming the 4-1 aggregate win which booked Portsmouth's passage into another Wembley final, this time against Newcastle United.

Pompey had slipped to 11th in the league after 24 matches, but with the upcoming final in London for Redknapp, he had managed to recruit the out of favour Chelsea duo of Joe Cole and John Obi Mikel, the former of which he had nurtured through his days at Upton Park.

Cole didn't fail to disappoint as he scored in the League Cup final for Portsmouth on the way to a 2-1 victory over Newcastle which was settled by who else but Peter Crouch who dwarfed Jermain Defoe not only in stature but in his goal return for the past season.

In fact, Crouch was competing directly with Chelsea's Didier Drogba for the season's Golden Boot award and after the England international netted a double in his 27th match against Stoke, Crouch had moved to 21 goals in 27 games, whilst Drogba had struck on two fewer occasions but having only played 18 matches.

Didier Drogba's over a goal a game ratio would help lift Chelsea to a third Premier League title under Roman Abramovich but with Portsmouth only retaining a top half finish by the skin of their teeth, Peter Crouch hadn't bagged the goals necessary to overtake his Ivorian counterpart in the scoring charts.

One thing that 'The Drog' didn't have to his name at the end of May 2010 was a European final to attend. Crouch was profusely scoring for Portsmouth, especially in Europe where his seven goals in his past five knockout round ties had helped Pompey through the likes of Wolfsburg, Hamburg and even Juventus in the semi-finals.

Atletico Madrid awaited Pompey in the Volksparkstadion in Hamburg but it wasn't Peter Crouch who would deal the crucial blow to the Spaniards in Germany. It would be Jermain Defoe, who had been out of form but continuously trusted by Redknapp who would net the decisive double which would sink the Spanish as Portsmouth won their third cup competition in as many seasons, completing a domestic and European cup double in 2010.

It wouldn't be all plain sailing for Redknapp, however, as the big-money signing of Lukas Podolski from F.C. Koln for around eleven million pounds in June 2010 rattled through the sports newsrooms around the country, Jermain Defoe refused to signed a new contract, after Podolski had scored the winning goal in a World Cup second round tie in Bloemfontein earlier in the month, to knock England out of the tournament.

Defoe would be shipped off to Valencia for a measly six million, but he wouldn't be sorely missed.

Financed by a mixture of Defoe's departure and the winnings from the two cup wins earlier in the year, Redknapp recruited some steady heads into his side, he snatched Vincent Kompany from under the noses of Arsenal before snapping up Darren Fletcher for nine million prior to an opening day at Fratton Park which didn't exactly mirror last season's.

Bristol City were newly promoted and along with Portsmouth would be the subject of Sky's first live Premier League broadcast of the new season which wouldn't end well for the home fans. With just four minutes on the clock, Vincent Kompany was red carded for a stomp on Lee Trundle before Peter Crouch put through his own net in an embarrassing 1-0 loss.

Ten undefeated games and a winning run in Europe, however, and Portsmouth were flying high by November. Redknapp's side would saunter through the group stages in Europe before briefly claiming second place in the league on Boxing Day with a memorable 2-1 away win at the Emirates Stadium, which left Arsenal seven points adrift of fourth place.

Vincent Kompany was becoming a leading light in the Portsmouth side and captained the side to an incomparable night in the Stadio Olimpico. Portsmouth had beaten Rome in the quarter final of the Europa League at Fratton Park, running out 3-1 winners but just two minutes into the return leg in Rome, Francesco Totti struck home a free-kick, leading to a nail-biting defensive display. The match summed up as Daniele de Rossi struck the post from a yard out before the midfielder was denied by a diving header from Kompany, as the Belgian blocked a ferocious shot with his own face.

The respect didn't relent for Kompany from his now adoring fans and it showed as the defender got the equaliser at home to Fulham which had Portsmouth cemented in the top five at least, going into the final three matches of the season.

European glory wouldn't swing around for the second time in as many years as Bayern Munich, fuelled by Champions League disappointment, hit Pompey for six in Munich after a resilient 0-0 on the south coast in the semi-finals of the Europa League.

Successive draws against Stoke and Newcastle did nothing to soothe the nerves of Portsmouth fans, as only a point separate them from Chelsea and Arsenal, who were akin to sharks sniffing blood. Portsmouth would be paired against Middlesbrough on the final day, needing a win at the Riverside to be sure of a place in the Champions League in the 2011-12 season.

Redknapp stocked his men well, Portsmouth ran out 3-0 winners in the North-East which rendered Arsenal's 2-1 win over Aston Villa useless, whilst Chelsea struggled to a 2-2 draw against Blackburn. In the away end the Portsmouth fans were visibly jubilant but the win would reap severe consequences for their opponents Middlesbrough, whose supporters jeered them as they exited the field of play, being relegated. Two years later, Middlesbrough would plummet to League One, the third tier of English football.

Redknapp described the Champions League as the "prime focus point" for the new season as Pompey initiated the new season, gaining just two points from the opening five matches in the league but with Lukas Podolski rejuvenated, the German forward put Portsmouth into a first-half 2-0 lead away at the San Siro against Inter Milan. They would win the tie in Italy, before beating Borussia Dortmund at home and achieving four points against BATE Borisov. The south-coast club topped Group G after the opening four games but a huge 4-0 defeat at Fratton Park to

Inter Milan they were in need of a win at the Signal Iduna Park, a fearsome place to go, and the home of the ever-growing Borussia Dortmund.

Robert Lewandowski's first half goal surged the home side into a 1-0 lead which they would only surrender when Dortmund's German counterpart and tormentor-in-chief, Lukas Podolski notched up another two Champions League goals, taking his tally to six from as many games as a 2-1 win over Dortmund was sufficient to seal their passage to the knockout round.

Forty-eight hours had passed and Redknapp was sat in Portsmouth's representative seat in a building in Nyon, Switzerland, awaiting the second round draw for the Champions League. His face lit up when Porto was retrieved from the hat, Redknapp could smell blood.

Short-lived domestic cup campaigns left Redknapp to concentrate on retaining their Champions League rights for the following season and in February, Portsmouth looked to set to achieve exactly that. As a Pompey fan, the successive matches thrown at them with the likes of Liverpool, Chelsea and Arsenal, the fixture list looked daunting towards the back end of the season but a shocking 1-0 win at Stamford Bridge coupled with back-to-back victories at Fratton Park over the other two aforementioned clubs left Portsmouth in second place with ten matches remaining.

Another competition Portsmouth were excelling in was Europe's top table – the mighty Champions League and a plucky 2-2 draw in Portugal granted Portsmouth as the favourites with the bookmakers. Porto seemed dishevelled at Fratton Park in the return leg, Peter Crouch was making a nuisance of himself in the air and with the aerial threat it was only a matter of time until Crouch netted Portsmouth's opener. Porto would level the match up late on but it wasn't enough as Portsmouth recorded their first last eight appearance in any European competition.

Waiting for them in April, however, was Real Madrid and the Bernabeu. The only English club to win away at Real Madrid was Arsenal a few years previously but Redknapp could not share the same anecdotes with the press in the post-match interviews as his Portsmouth side were effectively dumped out of the competition, losing 5-1 and having Vincent Kompany sent off left his side a little short going into the second leg.

Real Madrid drew another European full house in Fratton Park and with most of the fans, except the stubborn die hard supporters, without the hope of qualification, Portsmouth went all out to give their flocking supporters a memory they wouldn't forget and that memory was a 1-0 victory thanks to a late Lukas Podolski goal. Real Madrid would defeat Manchester United in the final in Munich, completing a double which included the Spanish La Liga, whilst in turn thwarting Manchester United's treble attempt.

Portsmouth would achieve third place in the Premier League but not before the looming departure of a certain Fabio Capello as the England manager would leave the side after months of intense negotiations after England's failure to qualify for the European Championships for a second successive time.

The rumour mill ran into overdrive across the summer as Spain romped home to yet another European Championship title with Harry Redknapp being declared the new England manager in waiting by the tabloids, in preparation for World Cup qualifying.

Redknapp would go onto solidify his position at Portsmouth by signing young defender Mats Hummels along with Sergio Busquets, speaking of an "evolving" Portsmouth and that the only constant for the "foreseeable future" being himself. The tabloids did not relent, however, until Stuart Pearce was announced the new England manager by the Football Association. Pearce would be unemployed within a year.

The League Cup and FA Cup was banished from Portsmouth's programme in the 2012-13 at the third round stage, the earliest possible elimination. A small portion of fans grew restless of Portsmouth's constant failure in domestic cup competitions but as Portsmouth topped both their Champions League group and the Premier League come the end of November.

The limited disappointment within the Portsmouth supporters was quelled somewhat with the marquee transfer in the January window as David Beckham exchanged Los Angeles for Portsmouth, after a successful season at the Galaxy in the MLS.

The rebound from January was vicious by Portsmouth, as they opened the month and the year of 2013 with a 3-0 home loss to Liverpool and with a further four losses in January and the earlier parts of February was banished thanks to seven successive Premier League wins.

These wins were only matched with two victories over Shakhtar Donetsk in the second round followed by an away goals triumph against Liverpool in two fiery quarter final encounters that had Portsmouth supporters dreaming of a final appearance with their love affair at Wembley.

Bayer Leverkusen were their semi-final opponents, once more Harry Redknapp smelled blood. A 2-0 loss at the BayArena had Pompey fans worried but were fuelled by the previous night's win for Arsenal over Barcelona, an all-England final was a desperate promise from the Fratton Park following.

A quick-fire double from Peter Crouch levelled the tie up as early as the sixth minute. A spanner would be implemented by the Germans when Andre Schurrle got the vital away goal which left Crouch and Portsmouth needed another two progress into the final. A Mats Hummels header warranted the hope from Portsmouth with an 81st minute goal. The night, however, belonged to Peter Crouch who netted the third of his hat-trick goals, progressing Portsmouth through to the final, 4-3 on aggregate. The robot was dusted down and performed by the England forward as Portsmouth would revel in their glory all night.

Portsmouth had to plough through Premier League before any possible Champions League success was to be guaranteed. On the final day, Portsmouth led the champions, Manchester United by two points needing a win over Stoke City at the Britannia Stadium. Peter Crouch would snatch a last-gasp equaliser in the Potteries in a 1-1 draw, leaving Manchester United to win by four clear goals at home to West Ham United; they would go onto win 6-1.

After having probably his best chance at a Premier League cruelly ripped away from him, Harry was on a manhunt for the Champions League in a self-described "all or nothing clash" for the Portsmouth manager. With a 40,000 strong Pompey contingent inside Wembley stadium, Lukas Podolski's goal launched Portsmouth into a second half lead. Arsenal were the strongest side throughout and perhaps deserved their 73rd minute equaliser through Thomas Vermaelen. The already tense match was thrown into the drama of extra time and a successful season had been thrown into turmoil in a matter of six days as the terrific acquisition of a few seasons gone by in Vincent Kompany put through his own net, gifting Arsenal's first Champions League to Arsene Wenger in 2013.

The disappointing climax to the 2012-13 season combined with the love affair for his dream job as the England boss, Harry Redknapp replaced Stuart Pearce just five days after the Wembley heartache. Portsmouth named a stand after Redknapp in his honour, with many pundits calling time on Portsmouth's glory years. They would be dumped out of the Champions League group stages at the hands of Rafael Benitez who would gift Portsmouth the League Cup in 2014 but transformed them back into a club flirting with relegation just two years later before his sacking upon Portsmouth's relegation at the end of the 2016/17 season.

Harry Redknapp, however, moved swiftly into the opposite direction, coaching England to an undefeated World Cup qualifying campaign with his one and only loss as England manager coming in the semi-final against Argentina in the 2014 World Cup, he subsequently retired from football management on a high.

3

David Beckham: England Manager

David Beckham is possibly the most famous footballer of his generation due to the high-profile nature his life is lived through the media, his football ability and how, worldwide, everyone has been exposed to 'Brand Beckham'. His famous right foot exploded onto the scene with a long-range effort from the inside of his own half in August 1996 against Wimbledon and gained plaudits for his crossing and free kicks among other things in his earlier days at Manchester United. Just two years later he became a household name for all the wrong reasons, receiving a red card for kicking out at Diego Simeone in a World Cup second round match. Burning effigies were pictured and published by the press but the hatred within the country would only wane following Manchester United's treble-winning campaign in 1999, which featured a quarter final win over Simeone's Inter Milan.

Beckham had become one of the first names on the England and Manchester United team sheet. He picked up six Premier League winners medals in his time at United with a couple of FA Cups to his name too. He drew criticism from the press after giving England fans the finger in response to their colourful selection of chants directed towards Beckham following their 3-2 loss against Romania which consequently eliminated them from the European Championships in 2000. However, Beckham would once again come out of a poor international tournament smelling of roses. Peter Taylor, England's caretaker manager handed him the captaincy before Sven-Goran Eriksson gifted him the armband permanently throughout the 2002 FIFA World Cup campaign and beyond.

In 2003, Beckham moved to Real Madrid, joining the Galacticos, winning the La Liga title whilst captaining his country right up until the conclusion of the 2006 FIFA World Cup when Steve McClaren was named England's new manager, and we all know how sour that reign turned out to be. All in all, Beckham captained England 59 times, whilst sitting second on the list of all-time appearances for the national side, only behind Peter Shilton, after making his final appearance in a World Cup qualifier in October 2009 in a 3-0 win over Belarus before his heel injury ruled him out of the subsequent tournament in South Africa. He still holds the record for the most England international appearances for an outfield player on 115.

Beckham wouldn't play at a tournament again after their successive exits in the European Championships and World Cup in 2004 and 2006 to Portugal via penalty shootouts whilst England's failure to qualify in 2008 under McClaren and through injury at the 2010 World Cup halted his participation. The former United winger would assist Capello in South Africa as a coach and slightly miss out on participation as part of Team GB for the 2012 Olympics through a decision made by manager, Stuart Pearce.

He wouldn't be selected for Euro 2012 as part of new manager Roy Hodgson's squad selection for the European Championships, stating in an interview after the World Cup in 2010 that he'll never retire from international football. To boost any slim hopes of ever playing for the national side again under Hodgson he signed for Paris Saint-Germain in January 2013, on a six-month contract. At this point in time, Hodgson was preparing his squad for a titanic battle against minnows San Marino for a World Cup qualifying match, of which they were 2nd in their group, behind Montenegro, their other opponents in March of 2013. Beckham would retire his playing career, becoming a Chinese football ambassador in the summer of 2013.

Let's enter the story prior to the European Championships in Poland and Ukraine in 2012. **David Beckham joins the England coaching staff instead of his long-time friend, former team mate and best man at his wedding, Gary Neville.**

Beckham sits by throughout the European Championships in 2012, unable to quell England's exit from the tournament in the quarter finals thanks to yet another penalty shootout loss to Italy, with Ashley Young and Ashley Cole missing decisive penalties. Several tabloids throughout England's subsequent seamless run in the World Cup qualifiers had reported that there was an air of tension around the England camp, labelling Beckham as Hodgson's successor and how Beckham was supposedly furious at the lack of penalty practice during the build-up to the Italy match.

David later denied these claims made by the tabloids in a press conference after the 2014 World Cup in Brazil. That press conference was to announce himself as the England manager, many in the media thought that this was the right move for England as Beckham knew the side inside out and with a recent fulfilled playing career fizzling out at PSG, he had the knowledge to take England to the European Championships in 2016 and win.

Hodgson ceremoniously handed the reigns over to the former England captain at the press conference in Rio de Janeiro after their humiliating 2-1 loss in the second round of the tournament to Poland. The hype was building ferociously around Wembley for the August friendly match with Cameroon but an ageing England were put to the sword 3-2 in their own backyard. This time, the media weren't too quick to jump the gun, as an international hero, they would give the new England manager time to settle in his first managerial job.

England looked all but qualified for the European Championships in 2016 after a 6-1 win over Moldova in September 2015, with Danny Welbeck rattling in his first England hat-trick. Tricky away matches were approaching in Serbia and Wales but England surprisingly led Holland in the standings by a couple of points. That deficit was cut as Holland demolished Bulgaria and England were unable to penetrate the immovable Serbia in Belgrade.

A month later and the Battle of Britain ensued on the hallowed Millennium Stadium turf in Cardiff which saw an early Gareth Bale goal that ensured England were chasing the game right from the fourth minute. Wayne Rooney came off the bench following knee surgery to pick up a last-gasp equaliser which kept England in touch with Holland awaiting their showdown three days later at Wembley.

However, Beckham's inexperience in the job was telling as his gamble on Rooney's inclusion gained a point but it would be later announced that he would be injured for a year with a torn cruciate ligament, he would miss the European Championships in 2016.

Beckham was preparing himself for play-offs should it be necessary as Wales only needed a win over Moldova to leapfrog England, should the Three Lions lose to Holland. Third place meant play-off heartache and the possible dreaded shootout, but in actual fact, a sumptuous display from a man widely thought to be too old for the international game squeezed England through as group winners.

Frank Lampard was plying his trade at LA Galaxy after failure to reach a contract agreement with Chelsea in the summer of 2014 and his two goals and further assist help sink Holland 3-0 in a display of similar magnitude to their 4-1 win at the same ground some nineteen years previous in the 1996 European Championships.

After the scintillating performance, Lampard announced his retirement from international football after the European Championships in France in the summer, leaving the likes of Tom Cleverley and Jack Wilshere stood like vultures waiting to snap up his position in the first eleven.

Wales would qualify via the play-offs and would be drawn in Group C of the European Championships, alongside David Beckham's England, Slovenia and Sweden. Danny Welbeck who had netted 27 league goals in the previous season for Manchester United was continuing his form into the international tournament, scoring four times in the group stages which saw England dominate, becoming one of only two sides in the group stages to carry an unblemished record into the second round.

Bosnia were the minnows awaiting them in the second round and Welbeck added another to his tally before an unlikely double from Steven Caulker who was standing in for the injured Gary Cahill.

Snapshots in the four days leading up to a quarter final against the hosts in France saw Beckham's side going through penalty drills throughout the entirety of the morning before kick-off. These pictures from the tabloids would come in handy to prove Beckham's status as a good manager which had been a simmering debate in the media throughout the tournament, that is, if they could win their first shootout in two decades.

Caulker missed England's fourth penalty but with a crucial miss from Jeremy Menez, Ashley Young was allowed to erase the demons from four years previously, almost tearing the net apart as England won the shootout 4-2. Another knockout match came and with Beckham's now famous penalty techniques instilled, England would surely show their hand again after another gruelling 120 minutes of goalless football.

Would the exposure from the British tabloids benefit Roberto Mancini's Italy? Would Mancini know the traits of the players from his time in England? And, most importantly, could England pull off another "once in a blue moon" penalty shootout win. A 4-1 win with dramatics from Joe Hart to save two had England into their first tournament final in half a century. The picture that graced *The Sun*'s back page the following morning was Beckham lifting Hart on his shoulders, akin to Bobby Moore's celebration with the Jules Rimet Trophy at Wembley in 1966, with the headline splashed underneath, a message that would conjure up all the determination in the fans for the Sunday encounter in the Stade de France: "Bring on Spain!"

As *The Sun* predicted, Spain were the opponents after a 5-0 drubbing of Germany in the semi-final and in the hope of a third successive Euro crown, Danny Welbeck dashed those Spanish dreams with his fifth goal in the opening thirty-seven seconds to give England a priceless lead in the tournament final.

Spain huffed and puffed and finally blew the sturdy England defensive brick wall down, agonisingly, in the final five minutes as Jordi Alba headed home for the Spanish opponents. This left Beckham able to re-group his side, and head into a third successive extra time period.

The commentators from both the BBC and ITV both questioned England's endurance to get through a third successive 120 minutes in a matter of eight days. It was Welbeck v Torres in terms of the golden boot and Torres got the cruel goal on the stroke of half-time which left England needing a minor miracle to win the contest outright.

The Three Lions had limped through the latter stages of the tournament but the roar could be heard from the white half of the Stade de France as Tom Cleverley's audacious effort eight minutes from time caught Iker Casillas unawares as England equalised, looking to force another penalty shootout.

The now iconic images can be seen in the National Football Museum in Manchester and at the St. George's Park National Football Centre in Burton-on-Trent of David Beckham intruding onto the pitch, urging his men to go forward, even physically pushing Ashley Young further upfield and waving Joe Hart to clear his lines up to his reliable front men.

This instruction paid off as a wobbly Spanish defence failed to cut out Hart's route one clearance which evaded Gerard Pique and with the slightest of touches, Welbeck guided the ball through Casillas' legs before accelerating past the legendary goalkeeper to tuck the ball away in the final moments of the match, gifting both the golden boot for himself and the European Championships for the entire nation with two neat touches of a football. England had ended their fifty years of hurt.

England were confident of World Cup success and only second in the FIFA World Rankings behind Argentina, they sauntered through the qualification for the Russian World Cup in 2018 with an unharmed record, conceding only two goals in a 4-2 victory over Slovakia in Bratislava in September 2017.

They were being dubbed as the favourites to win the tournament not just by the British media, but by the world's media. England graced a side full of promising young talent as well as stars at the peak of their game. The Wayne Rooney and Danny Welbeck combination shown for Manchester United in the previous few seasons which had warranted a couple of Champions League trophies was sure to lead England to at least the final in Moscow.

A 3-1 loss inspired by new Portugal coach Luis Figo dented England's hopes with a last gasp Phil Jones header only saving them from major embarrassment against Honduras a couple of days later. The Democratic Republic of Congo were the last side remaining in Group G, the England fans that approached the stadium that day weren't in the jovial mood that they were in anticipation of the clash with Spain in the Euro 2016 final or even the previous week against Portugal.

Four Danny Welbeck goals coupled with a 40-yard Wayne Rooney screamer among others, led England into the second round of the tournament on goal difference ahead of Honduras in an 11-0 thrashing which didn't have England fans foaming at the mouth just yet, but they were still confident of progressing with ease past Tunisia in the knockout stages.

England and Tunisia traded two goals in the opening ninety minutes but extra time, where England had shone so famously in the previous tournament, was their downfall in Russia. Three goals from the African nation either side of half time had the Three Lions and David Beckham shell-shocked beyond all recognition. England had six forwards up front but they couldn't defy a Tunisia side that would be obliterated by eventual champions Brazil in the quarter finals.

Beckham, before a host of the world's media, vowed to stay on as the England manager as he battled through a tough press conference. Beckham hadn't reached his low point as the England manager just yet, that would come in a few months' time. A win over Belgium kicked off the European Championships 2020 qualification campaign very well, but with successive losses over Ireland and Ukraine at Wembley, England were in the middle of the table, and three points off the play-off place with almost half of the qualification wrapped up.

A 2-1 win over Scotland did England some good in November, but it didn't quell the rage from the supporters and journalists afterwards in a tight contest which England should've dominated at Wembley. The following March, with San Marino claiming their first ever competitive win, at Wembley to boot. David Beckham looked a shell of his former self as the England manager as he could be seen wiping away a tear or two as he exited the stadium, the onslaught of the Wembley crowd heard after the 1-0 loss.

Beckham took a UEFA fine for not attending what would have been a tumultuous post-match press conference but an uninspiring 0-0 draw at Hampden Park against Scotland left England needing a miracle to qualify, and also a new manager. Six points off the second automatic qualification place and five off the play-off place, England were in fifth position, only behind their conquerors San Marino, England were looking down and out.

Gary Neville, who was overlooked for the European Championships in 2012 to guide Roy Hodgson as a coach, was elected as the new manager after a successful four-year stint at Inter Milan.

Neville didn't make sweeping changes but it was apparent by September came around that there was a new, determined mind set around the England camp. England cut down deficits with wins over Belgium and Ukraine in September before an inspired Alex Oxlade-Chamberlain performance in Dublin helped England to a 4-1 win over Ireland and subsequently landed England second place in the group, with their superior head-to-head over Belgium squeezing them into the European Championships.

Under Neville, there was a rehabilitated optimism and the nation's media surprisingly took well the appointment of David Beckham as his new assistant manager in the build-up to the tournament in Italy. England were being touted as second favourites behind Spain, an all too familiar danger zone for England managers and players in the past where over-confidence from the nation's journalists was shot down early on in the tournament by under-par performances.

A 1-1 draw with Poland meant very little in the grand

scheme of things as a win from the next two games would qualify them in either second or third place. However, Danny Welbeck announced himself further on the international scene in five days which changed his entire career. Back-to-back hat-tricks in wins over Croatia and Portugal not only powered England to the top of the group but landed Welbeck with a six-year contract at Real Madrid, in a forty-three million pound transfer, dragging him away from his beloved Manchester United.

Welbeck would get the goal in a gruelling second round contest with Germany which would solidify not only successive golden boot awards at the tournament but England's place in the quarter finals, where Neville's England dispatched Croatia again as they seemingly rampaged to the final again.

Italy awaited in the semi-final but headlines prior to the match were being written on the back pages about Italian hooliganism, and not about Welbeck's eight-goal tournament. Worse was to come, as England entered the San Siro with an-all Italian backing in the stadium, there were murmurs that Italy had filled the stadium twelve hours before kick-off with Italian fans in a desperate Government ploy as the Italians craved a trophy after fourteen years of hurt since Zidane's headbutt gifted them the World Cup in 2006.

The occasion seemed to lift Neville's men where the some 80,000 Italians announced themselves on the semi-final, in the cauldron-like atmosphere. The Italians lit their blue flares and the haze of the smoke bombs warranted opposition from Gary Neville and his incessant screaming at the players but the mist would cloud over a glossy English victory. Raheem Sterling scored the winning goal where the only celebration emanated from the England bench and the England players in an eerie moment which was rapidly becoming the soundtrack on a shameful night for Italy and Italian football, shortly condemned by the world's media and the footballing governing bodies for their underhandedness. They would be banned from 2022 World Cup qualification and FIFA consequently fined the Italian FA upwards of 200,000 euros.

The semi-final night would be remembered for the solitary goal which warranted the jubilant England celebrations throughout the bars and restaurants across Milan that evening, it became the night which Gary Neville turned Milan English, whilst the Italians were all crammed into the San Siro.

The Olympic Stadium awaited the now titanic clash between England and Spain, a repeat of the previous final but one where Gary Neville outshone Carles Puyol in tactical terms, dominating a Spanish side, in a reversal of roles from the Stade de France contest some four years previously.

An early Jack Wilshere goal had Spain rocking before whom else but Danny Welbeck fired England into a two-goal lead which would gift England a successive European Championship which took Joe Hart to the all-time highest appearance holder for England as he lifted the Henri Delaunay trophy again as the captain.

Upon his retirement from coaching a few years later, Beckham, for his efforts was knighted before the Queen for his philanthropy and his services to football, especially through the managerial side, with Gary Neville continuing England's reign of terror at the top of the international game, in wait of his knighthood when he retired.

4

The West Yorkshire Samba Beat

Let's face it; Pele is in everybody's top footballers of all time. One of only a rare collection of players to net over a thousand goals in his professional career, however, Pele was never able to tear himself away from the Americas and was never tested in the more competitive waters of European football.

That niggling doubt will always allow entry for Diego Maradona into the debate of the world's best footballer and Maradona was in fact named FIFA's Player of the Century ahead of the Brazilian talisman in 1999 thanks to a FIFA internet poll. Maradona's successful spells at top outfits such as Barcelona and Napoli throughout the 1980's and early nineties at the height of his powers always factors in the Argentine's advantage.

Pele only ventured out of Brazil and transferred from his beloved Santos in 1975 when he came out of semi-retirement to boost New York Cosmos' popularity and attendances in the late seventies. Pele is the only player in the history of football to collect three World Cup winners' medals which is a distinct advantage over Maradona's solitary title in 1986, which featured an infamous left-hand and, four minutes later, a weaving run which resulted in the now-dubbed "The Goal of the Century" in a quarter-final occasion with England.

After the 1990 World Cup final disappointment, Maradona was still in search of nearing Pele's World Cup triumphs in what was planned as a 1994 swansong. Controversy would de-rail the hopes of a second title for the Argentines after he was removed from the squad and suspended following the discovery of illegal substances in his system after scoring one of the goals of the tournament against Greece in a 4-0 win in Foxborough.

One of the biggest debates in the history of football concerns the superiority between Pele and Maradona. On one hand, Maradona's controversy held him in a different regard to the innocent and successful Pele, who was untested in the big leagues of Europe. **What if Pele signed a contract agreement prior to the 1958 World Cup, signing for Huddersfield Town on his 17th birthday, in October 1957?**

Huddersfield Town announced the capture of the young Brazilian starlet, Pele at their Leeds Road stadium on 26th October 1957, who was dubbed the future "greatest player in the world" just a year previously and had already notched up a goal a game in Brazil for Santos.

Pele's opening venture into British football wouldn't come until the middle of November on a snowy trip to Grimsby where many in the media were on the prowl, ready to criticise the incoming talent, who apparently wasn't prepared for the conditions at hand and hadn't experienced the wintery Britain prior to this contest.

The foot of snow was cleared from the turf in Grimsby, just in time for Pele to doubt all of his critics whom swamped the ground prior to kick-off. The back pages would be written by the five goals that Pele netted in a dominating display in a 6-0 win.

Huddersfield were languishing in 12th place in the Second Division prior to Pele's acquisition but he soon reached fifteen goals in a Terriers' shirt after only six games which featured three hat-tricks against Leyton Orient, Bristol Rovers and Doncaster Rovers. Town soon felt that they would gain promotion with their new boy wonder at the top of his game.

Pele would go onto score an almost unprecedented 52 times in three quarters of a season, with Dixie Dean applauding Pele's efforts of almost surpassing his record for goals in a season which Dean accomplished with Everton, netting sixty times just thirty years previously in 1928. With almost two goals a game in the blue and white of Huddersfield, Pele received a call-up from the yellow and blue of his nation for the FIFA World Cup in Sweden.

Two goals against Austria in a 5-1 win on the opening day of the 1958 games was a mere fraction of an introduction to the world of Pele's ability. He didn't find the net in the next match against England but was instrumental in a 2-0 win, assisting Vava in his two goals before finding the net again in a 3-1 win over the Soviet Union as Brazil completed the group stage with the only perfect record of the tournament, and had now become the tournament favourites with the 17-year old talisman up at the top of the park.

Wales were the quarter final opponents in Gothenburg for Brazil and the match was turned on its head with a sublime piece of skill from the man of the moment which foreshadowed the 'Goal of the Century' from Maradona in 1986. The Brazilian mastermind, as he was named after the winning goal against Wales was due to the trickery in which the forward bulldozed through a group of the onrushing Welsh defence before shimmying past the goalkeeper and winning the contest with a few simple touches of the ball in a slender 1-0 victory.

French forward and top goalscorer in the tournament with seven goals, Just Fontaine was ruled out for the rest of the tournament which allowed Brazil a safer passage into the 1958 World Cup final. On the other hand, Pele was able to equal the record in the tournament securing a first half hat-trick in a damning afternoon for French football in a 6-0 victory for the Samba side.

Pele would be preparing for a World Cup final against Sweden against the hosts at the end of June, on the same night that most 17-year olds would be preparing for exam in school but this man was a young student to the game of football.

On the 29th of June, 1958, the student became the teacher as he taught the Swedes a lesson in football, scoring both of Brazil's goals in a simple 2-0 win which secured Brazil's first World Cup title. Pele was given a rapturous welcome back to Brazil and, subsequently, England as Huddersfield were preparing themselves for their first season back in the top flight.

All of the press gathered from the Munich Air Disaster and the Busby Babes in the earlier throws of 1958 had evaporated and were distributed to the other side of the Pennines into Yorkshire where the lenses of the media were focused in on the World Cup winner in West Yorkshire. Pele, who had also won the golden boot with nine goals from six matches had turned the head of the footballing world to the rapidly growing Brazilian region of West Yorkshire.

Pele's first outing in the top flight of English football would be against Preston North End. Many of the British media were anticipating a good season from Preston after their second place finish in the previous season. The sunny August opening day afternoon in Lancashire was reserved for Pele as he almost single-handedly disassembled the high-fliers with two goals and a couple more assists in a huge 4-1 away victory on the opening day. Four more goals in three games against Newcastle United, Portsmouth and Luton Town had Huddersfield topping the First Division by the end of the month.

By the time the festive period had arrived and concluded, Pele was the division's top goalscorer, with 24 goals in 26 matches for the Brazilian who could even afford to miss a month out through a knee injury in December and still help Huddersfield to fourth in the division, trailing the likes of Wolverhampton Wanderers, Manchester United and Arsenal by just four points.

Bill Shankly was steering Huddersfield to success that they hadn't acquired since the three successive titles in the 1920s achieved by Herbert Chapman. They were vying for a place in the top four of the league and Pele was still on fire but with a few matches remaining in the season. Shankly was up against his former club Preston North End and had the chance to go second in the table with a win and consequently relegate the underachieving North End.

Shankly became a hero on the terraces of Deepdale as Pele's early equaliser was cancelled out and two subsequent second half goals surrendered Town's place in the top five as Preston pulled a couple of goals out of the bag with a 3-1 win which granted them survival for the upcoming season in the top flight.

Some retrospectively stated that Shankly delivered deliberately confusing messages so Preston could take the initiative in the match. Whatever the rumours claimed there was a definite shift of momentum at Leeds Road as Huddersfield took just one point from their last couple of matches, placing sixth in the division. Despite the promising outlook that Pele had gifted them it seemed Huddersfield had gathered from their first season in the top flight since the earlier part of the decade, there was an air of anger around the squad.

The conglomeration of the back pages in the British media was focused for a few weeks in June around Pele's future at Huddersfield Town as clubs from around Europe had apparently being monitoring his progress, with Real Madrid coming to the forefront, and being the favourites to claim his signature by the end of the summer.

Real had won the opening four European Cups with some ease and with the likes of Alfredo di Stefano and Raymond Kopa at the Spanish club, the addition of the Brazilian would go a long way to establishing themselves as a European powerhouse in the early years of the European Cup.

Huddersfield knew what they had at their disposal though and felt that they either needed a phenomenal amount of money or needed to keep him and his goals at the clubs if they were to become a powerhouse themselves, not just in England but in Europe.

Pele stated that he wanted to play out the rest of his career at Huddersfield, the combination between him and Denis Law had a profound effect on Huddersfield's new stature. Pele called Town a "likeable and growing club" in the English game. Real Madrid had been warned off by the time the new season started with a shocking, multi-million pound price tag slapped on the shoulders of Pele.

Many within the media stated that the phenomenal three million pound price tag on Pele would heap the pressure onto him and the rest of the West Yorkshire club. However, Pele dispelled the pre-season reports with back-to-back hat-tricks against Burnley and Manchester United, still working the magic between himself and Law. Shankly would then accept Liverpool's offer to manage them after much speculation in the off-season period.

What followed could have been Huddersfield Town's collapse as Juventus weighed in to match Pele's price tag of three million, which was spectacularly turned down by Bill Shankly before his departure, who managed to overrule the Huddersfield Town board. Pele would reach 18 goals in 12 matches in his final burst in the blue and white of Huddersfield, which took the Terriers to the summit of English football by the end of December. Bill Nicholson, after just one year in charge of Tottenham was snapped up by Huddersfield and two swift business deals were secured within the end of the first week of his management.

Juventus dramatically upped their transfer fee, splurging their entire budget to bring the young pretender to Turin, smashing the record transfer fee and breaking the million pound barrier, paying four-and-a-half million, breaking their own record of 93,000 pounds which they paid for Enrique Omar Sivori in 1957.

Pele joined up with Sivori and John Charles to create the Italian Holy Trinity in Turin and Juventus sauntered to their 11th Serie A title, beating Fiorentina to the title in 1960 by eleven points with Pele netting twenty goals in eighteen league games, overshadowing Sivori and Charles who got twenty-seven goals between them in a mouth-watering threesome which would go onto dominate Italian football for the next decade.

Meanwhile in Yorkshire, Huddersfield were stirring up their own collection of players. An unhappy John Charles was signed for 100,000 pounds at the end of the season in which Huddersfield claimed a respectable eighth place without Pele. A young 19-year old Bobby Moore joined Charles along with England forwards Jimmy Greaves and Dennis Viollet as Huddersfield secured the signings by spending only a fraction of the 4.5 million fee accumulated from Pele's sale.

Viollet's belated England career was established thanks to his signing at Huddersfield as he would go onto help them to a semi-final place in the 1962 FIFA World Cup with five goals. Juventus' Pele would, however, shine brighter. 1961 would be his and Juventus' year as they stemmed the Real Madrid dominance, beating them 3-1 in the European Cup final thanks to two late Pele goals in Berne.

Huddersfield were only a few points shy of their fourth English crown by the time Juventus were celebrating their 12th Italian title in 1961 but it was to be a 2-2 draw away at Sheffield Wednesday that helped Tottenham to a double-winning season, leaving Yorkshire hearts shattered.

Gordon Banks was a much needed addition to the Huddersfield ranks and helped Huddersfield, with a polished defensive record, to their fourth top flight English title whilst Pele scored seventy-three goals in the 1961-62 season, obliterating Dixie Dean's record, which was being compared in the media to Town's top goalscorer, Dennis Viollet's forty-two.

Juventus would shake off the Yorkshire comparison by claiming further titles with successive European Cup crowns whilst Pele would cement himself as a household name by netting a second World Cup title in 1962. After a stellar performance at the World Cup, Nicholson added more star power to the Leeds Road ranks. Bobby Charlton was added as well as the experienced Hungarian forward Ferenc Puskas for a whopping 1.7 million fee, eight years after he appeared in the 1954 World Cup final 3-2 loss to West Germany.

Huddersfield claimed their first league and cup double thanks to the combination of Law, Viollet, Puskas and Charles with the English backbone of Moore, Charlton and Banks which would secure further league titles in a 1960's dominated by the West Yorkshire blue and white of Huddersfield.

Juventus would be dominant on both fronts as Pele was fast approaching his thousandth goal, securing four European Cups in five seasons in the approach to the 1966 FIFA World Cup, hosted in England. Nicholson became a direct adviser to manager, Alf Ramsey in the build-up to the tournament.

Nicholson, who gifted Ramsey the now-experienced quartet of Viollet, Moore, Charlton and Banks, would receive wide recognition for the semi-final showdown between England and Brazil at Wembley on 26th July 1966, in the second greatest day of English football's national side history.

Bobby Charlton netted a first goal but Pele soon added his eighth and ninth goals of the tournament. Brazil looked too strong for England, Juventus too strong Huddersfield. Dennis Viollet got England's equaliser before the break but it would be a non-Huddersfield player in Jimmy Greaves, the Tottenham forward, who would get the decisive third and fourth goals in the 4-2 semi-final win.

Viollet would get the only goal in the 1-0 win over West Germany in a gruelling victory in England's first World Cup title—England's greatest day in footballing history. Huddersfield claimed their first European Cup in 1967, beating Benfica 2-0 in Ferenc Puskas' swansong, not before Juventus were beaten in the semi-finals thanks to a 5-3 aggregate victory by the Terriers. All four stands of the newly-refurbished Leeds Road cheered Pele off in a night which reduced the Brazilian man to tears.

Pele would win a further two European Cups, claiming ten Serie A titles in his career, retiring at Juventus in 1978 whilst Huddersfield Town would reach the summit of English football for the seventh time in 1976 which featured two FA Cups and a League Cup throughout the earlier parts of the seventies. Nicholson replaced Alf Ramsey as the England manager following failure to qualify for the 1974 FIFA World Cup, where Brazil upset the odds against Germany.

Pele would retire with four World Cup winners medals and three FIFA Golden Boot awards, Alf Ramsey and Bill Nicholson both received knighthoods in the nineties after steering England to World Cup success, with Nicholson's triumph coming in 1982, thanks to a Kevin Keegan brace against Italy in the final.

5

… and Shearer has won it

Alan Shearer is one of the biggest household footballing names in England, captaining the national side on many an occasion and being the all-time top goalscorer in the Premier League by a distance, with 260 goals. He claimed his solitary piece of silverware with the Premier League title in 1995 with Blackburn Rovers after signing from Southampton in 1992. His third and final club, Newcastle United, where he spent ten years from 1996 up until his retirement, obliterated the world transfer fee record of 15 million pounds which was held for three years before Nicolas Anelka signed for Real Madrid in August 1999. For a player of his stature, Shearer's career in terms of titles has to be seen as a disappointment because of all the class and goalscoring ability, Shearer could have added a lot more silverware than the solitary Premier League title along with multiple golden boot awards.

A semi-final appearance at the European Championships in 1996 was the closest he ever materialised any success with the national side he captained and he retired upon England's failure to reach the knockout stages of the same tournament four years later in the Netherlands and Belgium.

As the century turned, Shearer was coming no nearer the silverware he craved, with back-to-back FA Cup final defeats; it looked as though success was not on the CV of England's leading striker for a time. His thirty goals in sixty-three appearances for the national side places him at seventh in the rankings of the top goalscorers for the national team at the time of writing which granted him a place in the English football hall of fame in 2004 and has a pitch at the St. George's Park training facility in Burton-upon-Trent named in his honour.

Pele even named Shearer as one of 125 of the greatest living footballers in the same year as his hall of fame induction. He topped the Euro 96 goalscoring charts which warranted him the bronze award at the Ballon d'Or in the same year.

It is clear, that upon his retirement in 2006 that without the silverware in ten years at St. James' Park, even in the years of the late Sir Bobby Robson, the only thing missing from Shearer's résumé was silverware. The turning point in Alan Shearer's career was his move from Southampton to Blackburn Rovers in the summer of 1992 but the 3.3 of Jack Walker's millions managed to sway Shearer's decision away from Old Trafford and Alex Ferguson. Just two years later, Ferguson had guided Manchester United to successive Premier League titles and would later go onto dominate English football.

The English talisman claims to not regret the chance to play for what would be by the end of the decade the biggest club in world football. However, he has to wonder what if.

Alan Shearer plumps for Alex Ferguson over Kenny Dalglish and signs for Manchester United in the pre-season of the 1992-93 for a British record-breaking transfer fee of seven million pounds.

Ferguson unveiled two summer transfer window signings in the week prior to the opening Premier

League game against Oldham Athletic on 15th August 1992, with Eric Cantona joining Alan Shearer up front for the team photo. Mark Hughes still staked a claim in the side with a hat-trick on the opening day with both Shearer and Cantona chipping in with a goal each in the 6-1 victory at Old Trafford.

The media was lauding the new look trio at Old Trafford who would hit sixty-three goals between them in the Premier League's first season, with Shearer topping the goalscoring charts with a tally of 32 from 41 games, only missing one game all season. Cantona got seventeen goals from a deeper playmaking role and would be assigned the captaincy at United for the upcoming season with Mark Hughes on his way out to fellow Premier League side, Chelsea.

Alan Shearer would write himself into Old Trafford folklore in the forthcoming seasons as he netted 159 goals in his opening five seasons, averaging at over thirty a term. The offers were flying in from the likes of Arsenal, Juventus and Champions League holders, Real Madrid. With the ever-developing strike partnership of Cantona and Shearer, United would receive their long-awaited European glory in the 1998-99 season. Shearer was the favourite to net a fifth golden boot in six years whilst a sixth successive league crown was on the horizon.

The only frontier Alan Shearer was unhappy with was international success, and in an interview with *Football Focus* prior to the league match with Sheffield Wednesday at Hillsborough in November 1998, he wished for better structure for the England national team as Shearer's goals fired them into a World Cup quarter final where he couldn't add to his six goals in the tournament in a 2-0 loss to Holland who would go onto be defeated by France in the final in Paris.

Arsene Wenger and co. added to their group in North London with Dwight Yorke (Aston Villa) and Ole Gunnar Solskjaer (Chelsea) impressing for their respective clubs in the previous season and began the league campaign well. Arsenal continued their 100% record right through until November, winning their opening nine matches whilst United dropped four points in that period.

Shearer was leading the Arsenal trio in terms of goals but Eric Cantona wasn't living up to the expectations that preceded him in previous campaigns. There was a reported power struggle in the Old Trafford dressing room between captain-in-waiting Roy Keane and Eric Cantona. A few minor dressing room scuffles and on-field tantrums was only a mere calm before the storm when Arsenal travelled to Manchester United in what was billed as the match of the season by *Sky Sports*.

United fell to an early Patrick Vieira goal from the leaders as they threatened a seven-point lead with fifteen matches gone. Roy Keane was then felled in the penalty area from Lee Dixon and wished to take the subsequent kick to put United on level terms. Shearer and Cantona were amongst the candidates to take the kick but Roy Keane's ego got the better of him, physically shoving the two top goalscorers at the club aside to take the kick.

Shearer would back away almost instantly outside of the area but Cantona retaliated, lunging at the Irish midfielder who crashed to the ground. Alex Ferguson was quick to haul Roy Keane off, allowing Eric Cantona to take the penalty which was saved by David Seaman.

Cantona received a two-match ban whilst Roy Keane

was suspended for two months for the on-field drama as well as "a dressing room altercation" which Ferguson didn't go into detail with in the several post-match interviews.

Without the two key figures at United and an injured Teddy Sheringham, Ferguson was forced to stick youngster Erik Nevland up front for the key away ties at Middlesbrough and Newcastle. It was Shearer who would step up in United's time of need following the disappointing 1-0 loss at home to Arsenal. Nine goals in seven matches during Keane's suspension had overturned the deficit created in the earlier stages of the season by Arsenal and they led them by a point going into 1999.

United wouldn't falter again in the Premier League, coasting to an eleven-point lead by the time they lifted the trophy in early May with a 2-0 away win at Ewood Park, thanks to a brace from Alan Shearer who would finish the 38-match season with 34 league goals, a record.

The real competition for the Red Devils came in the form of the Champions League, Ferguson craved the title and United were looking for their second crown in the tournament, their first in thirty-one years since the 4-1 victory over Benfica at Wembley in 1968.

Shearer was absent through suspension and a subsequent injury for the quarter final ties against Inter Milan but Eric Cantona would step up and thanks to goals elsewhere coming from David Beckham, Paul Scholes and Ryan Giggs, United would almost casually saunter through to the final four, winning 6-2 on aggregate.

Alan Shearer returned for the home tie against Juventus and almost settled the tie on the spot with a first-half hat-trick. However, a late goal from Zinedine Zidane meant the berth in the final against Bayern Munich wasn't as sealed as Ferguson would've hoped.

Filippo Inzaghi's quick-fire double at the start of the second half in Turin meant United needed a goal, and within the half-hour. Roy Keane's marvellous header and commanding performance led him to take the captain's armband off Cantona for the subsequent season. This would add more unrest to an already unsteady outfit.

United would crawl through 4-3 on aggregate to a Nou Camp date in May against Bayern Munich who were chasing a Treble, as were United after defeating West Ham 4-1 at Wembley the previous weekend to win their fourth FA Cup in the nineties.

The final proved to be the easiest on the road to an unprecedented Treble in English football. Alan Shearer knocked in two close range goals to gift United their second European crown. A second would follow in 2001, on Eric Cantona's swansong as Alan Shearer, now inducted into the English football Hall of Fame thanks to his heroics for both the national side and Manchester United.

Cantona would wave goodbye to football at the San Siro and to the Manchester United fans after getting a goal in the 3-1 victory over Real Madrid. It was United and Shearer's first accolade since the 1999 Champions League trophy, the southern dominance had run throughout the Premier League.

Arsene Wenger added two successive Premier League titles to his tally as Dwight Yorke claimed successive golden boots as Shearer could only manage 37 league goals in two campaigns. After a trophyless season for the reigning European Champions and a group stage exit in the 2001-02 Champions League season, the foundations at Old Trafford collapsed from underneath them.

The newly-knighted Sir Alex Ferguson followed through with his retirement promise and sure enough, their star striker, Alan Shearer was sold on after becoming disillusioned after Ferguson's retirement and was sold onto their biggest rivals of the time, Arsenal, smashing a British transfer fee record of 32 million.

After ten successful years at Old Trafford, Alan Shearer would continue his trophy glut at Arsenal, and through the trio of Yorke, Bergkamp and Solskjaer, Shearer improved upon his treble at United by steamrolling through the entire league season undefeated, whilst his former employer finished in fourth position, the transfer of Andriy Shevchenko keeping United perilously afloat in terms of Champions League places.

Many pundits look back on the historic 2002-03 season from Arsenal and almost everybody can agree upon the turning point. It was 23rd April 2003 and Arsenal were going through a rough patch after being held to stalemates in their previous five league matches and only forcing their way into the FA Cup final through a penalty shootout victory over Bolton Wanderers at Villa Park.

They had surrendered their top place in the league to Newcastle with four matches remaining but one night Barcelona will be remembered by almost every Gunner fan not just in the stadium but throughout the world. Barcelona had triumphed 3-1 at Highbury thanks to a double from new signing Ronaldinho but Dwight Yorke was able to add a crucial goal heading into the second leg in northern Spain.

Barcelona edged further ahead in the second leg with another goal from the Brazilian which left Arsenal needing three goals to force extra time. Arsenal hearts were in their mouths as Barcelona had a perfectly good goal ruled out for offside on the stroke of half-time which would've altered Arsene Wenger's half-time plans somewhat.

The half-time whistle sounded and different stories have been told by different figures in the game, from the media, from past players who knew Arsene Wenger and from an assortment of players and staff inside the away dressing room in the Nou Camp. Whatever the stories might be, Wenger was severely annoyed and needed a win and he needed three goals to get Arsenal to extra time against an attack-minded Barcelona outfit.

Shearer would get two goals in the opening five minutes of the half which restored the belief in the away end of the stadium and around the smattering of pubs and bars across North London but it would ultimately be an old head that dragged Arsenal into extra time. Dennis Bergkamp would be gifted a goal by former Arsenal player Sylvinho and a fourth and vital goal in extra time fell to Alan Shearer who got his fortieth goal of the season in all competitions and fired Arsenal into a semi-final, not for the first time in the season.

Shearer claimed in a BBC interview a few years later that he had experienced a perfect footballing night—a hat-trick in a Champions League quarter final and an old enemy being put in their place. That old enemy was Manchester United who had taken a 1-0 lead to the Mestalla for their Champions League Quarter Final second leg in Spain. A place in the semis against Arsenal was ultimately at stake. However, the Red Devils had fluffed their lines, losing 4-0 in Spain to Valencia, the low point of their night came on the hour when Gary Neville put through his own net, allowing Valencia a vital second goal to pull them ahead on aggregate.

Arsenal would eliminate Valencia with two-goal wins in either leg which fed them A.C. Milan in the final at Old Trafford. Alan Shearer was back on his old stomping ground and two penalties were tucked away by the English international who was instrumental in the 3-2 win over the Italian side. Arsenal were consequently heralded as one of the greatest club sides in the history of football.

This was reaffirmed with yet another Champions League triumph in the subsequent season, Shearer netting 51 goals in all competitions as, with renewed optimism, he returned to the English national side for the European Championships in 2004, the side which had previously "lacked structure" had been apparently improved according to the Arsenal forward in what was being labelled prior to the tournament as the "golden generation" by the British tabloids.

Shearer was preferred to out-of-form Michael Owen up front in the opening match against France in Lisbon and would add to his international tally for the first time since the same tournament four years previously against Romania. England would be held 2-2 by France but the foundation was there for England to hit the ground running.

The combination between Shearer and Rooney was being declared as "out of this world" not just by the

British red-tops but by *L'equipe* and *Marca* who were camped in Portugal for the championships. The youngster, Wayne Rooney complimented the Arsenal forward well who would net a hat-trick against Switzerland in a 5-1 victory which also saw goals from David Beckham and the Everton talisman himself.

Shearer would add a fifth of the tournament in the slender 2-1 win over Croatia which put them top of the group, awaiting the hosts in the quarter finals.

Two further goals from Shearer would squeeze England through to their first major tournament final since 1966 after successive 1-0 victories over Portugal and Czech Republic which left minnows Greece in the final.

Some of the more foolish bookmakers were already paying out on an England tournament win. Angelos Charisteas had other ideas as he put Greece into a first half lead; England needed something from the tournament's star man. Michael Owen, who had recorded 37 minutes on the pitch throughout the entire tournament, was brought onto replace Wayne Rooney. Sven-Goran Eriksson was repaid almost immediately as the Liverpool forward linked up quickly with Alan Shearer before Owen pegged Greece back with 17 minutes on the clock remaining. Shearer would add a second some five minutes later before Owen sealed his hat-trick in a swift turnaround which saw England claim their first trophy with the 4-1 win over Greece.

Shearer would retire in 2007 after claiming a fifth Champions League winners' medal in Athens with a goal in the 2-0 win in the first all-English final against Liverpool before notching up three more Premier League crowns with Arsenal. To this day he remains as one of only two England trophy-winning captains alongside Bobby Moore and one of the most successful English footballers to have ever lived.

6

Turnip Taylor

Every coach has that one dream job but before Graham Taylor's England side was able to kick a ball under his management, the critics swooped in to create more of a nightmare for the two-time Watford boss.

There wasn't the excitement surrounding the new manager that an appointment often brings in football. Sadly, Taylor will only be remembered for failing to get England to the 1994 FIFA World Cup in the United States and not his opening spell of just one loss in his opening twenty-three matches in charge which was a loss against Germany at Wembley Stadium.

However, Taylor's England struggled to reach the European Championships in 1992, only qualifying ahead of Turkey, Ireland and Poland by the skin of their teeth which left supporters uninspired going into the tournament in Sweden. They were drawn against the hosts in the eight-team tournament with eventual winners Denmark and the former champions in France in Group A.

Taylor's stint in charge of the national side was coming off the back of key retirements to the likes of Peter Shilton and Terry Butcher. Two goalless stalemates against Denmark and France left England needing a victory against Sweden in what could've been Gary Lineker's final match in a Three Lions shirt should they be eliminated from the championships.

The Swedes were on top but the score remained tied

on the hour at 1-1 before Taylor pulled the worst possible rabbit out of the hat, hauling Gary Lineker off for Arsenal forward Alan Smith. This ultimately robbed Lineker of the chance of equalling Sir Bobby Charlton's international goal record of forty-nine goals but the former Leicester and Everton talisman would always be stuck one shy of the Manchester United legend.

Sweden would win the match and *The Sun* consequently published a super-imposed image of Graham Taylor wearing turnip features with the headline 'Swedes 2 Turnips 1' splashed across the front page. It wouldn't the last instalment of *The Sun's* 'Turnip Taylor' front pages.

Taylor came out to the country's media, admitting his mistakes post-tournament which restored his image in the country but after being held 1-1 by Norway, the media began to jump on the manager's back until three wins gave Taylor room to breathe. However, two successive draws to Holland and Poland before a post-season loss to Norway—all in qualification left England needing a miracle to qualify especially after going down 2-0 to Holland in the penultimate qualifier.

England were ready to wave away their World Cup dreams, as they relied on a Poland win in Poznan over favourites Holland and to beat San Marino but after just nine seconds, they were down against the Marinese minnows. Ian Wright would net a few goals in the 7-1 win for England but it wouldn't be enough after the Dutch sunk the Poles 3-1. Taylor would resign a week after failure to reach the World Cup.

What if Graham Taylor managed England to the 1994 FIFA World Cup? Poland beat Holland with an

early goal as England record a 7-1 away victory over San Marino in the final qualifying matchday.

Taylor was present for the World Cup draw in Chicago where England were pitted against their quarter final nemesis in Cameroon from four years previously along with debutants as a sole nation, Russia and three-time champions and favourites in Brazil. Paul Gascoigne was being put forward by the nation's media as their brightest hope to win the World Cup in the States and he didn't disappoint in the opener, getting a goal in a 4-0 win over Cameroon. Ian Wright would bag two in a brilliant outing for the Arsenal forward and he would get the only goal of the game against Russia which effectively put England through to the second round stage thanks to the 1-0 win.

A win over Brazil would have solidified Taylor as the England manager and a win over arguably the best footballing nation on the planet. They didn't have the best start in the Rose Bowl on 28th June 1994 as Romario opened the scoring and his account for the tournament within the three minute mark.

In the searing Californian heat, Taylor cut a sweaty and lonely figure as Brazil was playing them off the park in the opening forty-five. However, the former Watford man got the England side in the dressing room at half-time and for what the viewing public could tell from the following forty-five was that England were a changed team.

Ian Wright netted two quick-fire goals straddling the hour mark before a third and final header from Tony Adams sealed the three points and the perfect group record from Taylor, a transformation of epic proportions from the European Championships in

Sweden two years previously.

Many were now lauding the previously disparaged decision of Graham Taylor's to base England south of the border in Mexico prior to the tournament as they would face the hosts, United States in similar climates in California. Taylor's sweat was leaking from his pores which would mirror the host's defence as Paul Gascoigne netted a double in the 2-0 victory thanks to two major defensive second half mistakes when it looked as though England's Atlantic cousins could match them in a tournament scenario.

Taylor's sprint-celebration down the touchline smacked of relief to the viewing audience but it angered many of the host's supporters as he breached the touchline to celebrate with Gazza after the second vital goal, a picture which now dons the main entrance to the St. George's Park headquarters in Burton-upon-Trent.

The celebrations and post-match interview quirk from Taylor in which he labelled the hosts as a "nation not used to football" would spark a riot outside the ground after the full-time whistle between the two sets of supporters. The team bus would be attacked with bottles and stones by lurking American supporters after the match which drew more criticism from Graham Taylor.

The now-eliminated host nation was now pitted against England in their quarter final against Holland, where the Dutch outfit received a hefty new fan base for their crucial knockout tie against Taylor's England. David Platt would score a hat-trick to silence the large Dutch and American contingent inside the Cotton Bowl in Dallas where a 4-0 victory saw England safely through to successive World Cup semi-finals where they faced Romania, with a favourable chance of reaching their second World Cup, a first in twenty-eight years.

The scorching sun in the Rose Bowl in the semi-final blighted both Romania and England throughout the contest which resulted in a stalemate right up until the 88th minute when a teasing Gheorghe Hagi cross forced Stuart Pearce into a wayward clearance which found his own net, leaving England devastated and Romania facing their first World Cup final in their entire history where they were humiliated 6-1 by Italy in the final four days later. Meanwhile, England would receive further humiliation as their second string squad lost out to Bulgaria, 1-0 after extra time in the third-place play-off.

Despite reaching the semi-final *The Sun* still criticised Graham Taylor for his defensive tactics in the semi-final defeat to Romania. Whilst some outlets chose to praise Taylor for getting England to another semi-final, the expectation was definitely on England to win their first European Championship on home soil in two years' time.

Fast forward a couple of terms and Alan Shearer was on top form but had a niggling hip injury to worry about despite Ray Harford, his manager at Blackburn, stating he was match fit for the championships. Nonetheless, much to the scathing anger from the tabloids and supporters, Taylor plumped for Chris Sutton in the side ahead of Shearer who had finished the 1995-96 Premier League on top of the goalscoring charts.

Taylor still felt confident with Paul Gascoigne in the side and his loyalty looked to have repaid him with an early goal from the Rangers playmaker in the opener against Switzerland. England would go onto draw against the Swiss 1-1 before a visit from Scotland which ended in total humiliation, a 2-0 loss with both Steve McManaman and Chris Sutton both being sent off, becoming only the second and third England players to be sent off in a major tournament after Ray Wilkins in the 1986 FIFA World Cup.

Graham Taylor struck lucky as Scotland were held by Switzerland and an Ian Wright double against Holland either side of a Teddy Sheringham goal which was dubbed the goal of the tournament opened up a 3-0 lead which England cruised to, just about pulling themselves out of Group A and through to a quarter final against France.

Taylor's days as England manager were numbered, however, and after a poor group stage campaign, Chris Sutton returned to score the opening goal at Anfield against the French only for the likes of Zinedine Zidane, Youri Djorkaeff and Laurent Blanc getting goals on a dark day for English football, the French winning 5-1 on English soil, they would ultimately lose to Germany in the final at Wembley, with Graham Taylor sacked with immediate effect, on the other hand, for England.

England had better days ahead of them, qualifying for the 1998 World Cup, led by Terry Venables and would make it to their first FIFA World Cup final since Alf Ramsey and Bobby Moore led the English out to do battle with the Germans in 1966. However, Venables could only steer England to a 2-0 defeat to Brazil whilst Graham Taylor was watching the coverage on television, preparing for the 1998-99 season, in charge of Watford for a second stint. He would retire from football management after relegating Watford from the First Division in 2003.

7

The English Wizard

Ryan Giggs is held in high regard as one of the best footballers to have ever put on a Manchester United shirt and for such a big club it is a testament to the skill of the Welsh winger. Giggs recently completed his 1,000th professional appearance in a Champions League tie against Real Madrid and the once Ryan Wilson has appeared for Wales sixty-four times and even turning out for Great Britain at the Olympics at the 2012 London games. He has surpassed numerous record such as being the highest appearance holder for both Manchester United and the Premier League, scoring in all of twenty-one of the seasons, with a current streak of goals in every one of the past twenty-three seasons in the top flight.

Giggs, or Wilson as he was named at the time, played for England schoolboys once, scoring in his only under-16 appearance at Wembley. However, he turned out at every other under-age level for Wales. He was born to Welsh parents and ultimately chose to play for the Welsh national side and went onto make a total of no major national tournament appearances. He can pride himself for being on a list including the likes of Eric Cantona, Alfredo di Stefano, George Best and George Weah to never appear at a World Cup for one reason or another but it must eat at the famous number eleven that he could never grace the greatest stage of his sport.

The Manchester United winger who, at the time

writing, has collected thirteen Premier League winner's medals along with almost a handful of Champions League medals for his troubles, starting in four finals and winning half of them.

One can only wonder what else Ryan Giggs could have accomplished in his career had he have chosen English as his primary nationality when it came to football. On the other hand, there is a rumour that he couldn't have been selected for England in the first place.

As he continues to venture into the twilight stage of his career at Manchester United, remaining a one-club player and with the assortment of former United players who have gone into management, the lure of the World Cup could still be available to the man they call Giggsy on a coaching level in the not too distant future.

But for now, I'm asking, what if Ryan Giggs selected England as his primary nationality and was a permanent fixture for the senior national team across two decades?

Giggs was signed to a professional contract in November 1990 and made a name for himself almost immediately at Old Trafford netting his first goal in the Manchester derby in May 1991 but it wasn't enough to warrant him a place in

Alex Ferguson's Cup Winners' Cup winning final against Barcelona which would've been his first piece of professional silverware.

Lawrie McMenemy, the England under-21 coach would grant him a place in the side for the European Championship qualifiers against Poland and Turkey at the beginning of the 1991-92 season. He would produce a man of the match display at home to Turkey, netting twice before assisting in all three of England's goals in a 3-1 away win at Poland which effectively granted England qualification for the tournament in the summer of 1992.

Prior to the tournament, his exploits at club level earned him the 1992 League Cup with a win over Nottingham Forest in the final (his first of many trophies) and clinching the PFA Young Player of the Year award before leaving for the tournament. A win over Denmark fed England Italy in the semi-finals of the tournament but despite a free-kick from Giggs himself, they would go down 3-2 on aggregate to the Italians, who were the eventual winners thanks to a win over Sweden in the final.

Giggs was granted his first cap in the senior national side but was unable to help England in a 2-1 loss to Holland which knocked their confidence of qualifying for the 1994 FIFA World Cup. Giggs would make eleven more appearances in preparation for the European Championships in 1996, scoring twice after Graham Taylor's England couldn't secure qualification for the tournament in the United States.

The Manchester United winger had collected a couple of Premier League titles in the meantime and was competing directly with Liverpool winger Steve McManaman and Tottenham midfielder Darren Anderton for a starting eleven berth in the tournament.

Giggs made an impact coming off the bench in the opener against Switzerland, scoring the vital winning goal in a close encounter which England triumphed 2-1 at Wembley. He would be left out throughout the rest of the group stages as England progressed safely through victories against Scotland and Holland which left them with Spain in the quarter-finals and another substitution appearance, where Giggs replaced Anderton on the left-wing due to injury.

After the stalemate in the quarter-final at Wembley, the match was to be determined on penalties and after two spot kicks each, England led 2-1 and Giggs stepped up, calmly placing the ball past the goalkeeper as England went onto beat the Spaniards, with the Germans awaiting in the semi-finals.

Ryan Giggs made his first tournament start in an England shirt, playing from the left ahead of the injured Darren Anderton and assisting Alan Shearer for England's early opener in the third minute. Penalties would again decide England's fate after Stefan Kuntz's first half equaliser which Giggs replied to the supreme German penalty machine and duly converted, as well as four of his fellow England team mates. The same, however, couldn't be said for Gareth Southgate.

A successful pizza commercial later and Southgate was a superstar, Ryan Giggs was simply stuck with winning trophies, instead of the possibility of free Italian food. With the influx of English talent emanating from Manchester United, Ryan Giggs was becoming a permanent fixture in the English side, being an ever-present throughout a successful qualifying campaign for the 1998 World Cup in France, whilst performing at a high level both in England and Europe for his club side.

Three vital goals in the matches against Moldova and Italy got England over the line against the three-time world champions who proved their sternest opposition in a relatively easy qualifying campaign.

At the age of 24, Giggs was reaching his prime and

the 1998 FIFA World Cup was billed as his platform to go onto greater things, alongside David Beckham if he was given a starting berth by Glenn Hoddle. He made the plane to the tournament, preferred to David Batty, Paul Ince and Darren Anderton in the line-up and started the opener against Tunisia, assisting his club team-mate Paul Scholes in a routine opening win.

Giggs added to his tally of five England goals against Romania in a 2-2 draw which put England in prime contention to win the group with a win over Colombia. Instead, a goalless stalemate allowed Romania to sneak in under England's noses, leaving Giggs and co. with a tough task against the old enemy of Argentina.

A quick-fire first half allowed the world to realise the young talent of Michael Owen but it was Ryan Giggs who was labelled the hero, compared to the villainous status David Beckham achieved due to his red card for lashing out at Diego Simeone. Giggs would convert the decisive penalty in the shootout which set up a quarter final against the Dutch and Dennis Bergkamp.

The aforementioned Bergkamp would crush Ryan Giggs' dream of a World Cup at the first time of asking thanks to a stupendous goal, worthy of winning the World Cup, never mind a last eight match. They would go onto lose to Brazil in the semi-finals whilst the England team watched France pick up their solitary World Cup from their homes.

Fresh off an unprecedented Treble in 1999 and successive title victories with Manchester United, he was ready to strike fear into European hearts at the championships in Holland and Belgium, drawn in the group of death alongside Romania, Portugal and Germany. The winger was on a tally of eleven goals off fifty-eight appearances from his seven years in the senior national side.

Two goals in the 3-0 win over Portugal set England well on their way to recording a glorious European Championship campaign and further victories over Romania and Germany. Both Beckham and Giggs excelling as an outlet to Alan Shearer at the top of the park for England and the consistency of their strikers warranted a quarter final tie against co-hosts Holland.

The nation's media weren't questioning England's ability after nine goals off three games in the group stages but the ability to handle themselves at a major tournament against a top class opposition with a strong fan base in their own back yard.

Patrick Kluivert, who didn't feature in the quarter final win two years previously against England, netted an early goal which Michael Owen almost instantly cancelled out with an equaliser inside eight minutes. The game was balanced on a knife edge for half an hour, every kick meaning something, the tackles weren't exactly flying in but there was heart to the game, a great advert for European football.

Edgar Davids would split the game wide open in the five minutes preceding the first half, in one move he struck a goal from twenty-five yards and his next touch of the ball was to scoop a delightful chip over the entirety of the English defence, allowing Dennis Bergkamp a stab at goal, which resulted in Holland's third. England were tumbling unceremoniously out of a second successive tournament at the hands of the Dutch at the last eight stage.

A half-time Kevin Keegan team talk and a few harmless minutes later, Ryan Giggs provided a pass of complete genius. Dennis Wise rolled him the ball on the halfway line and with nobody aware of what was forthcoming, a single collection of the ball by the winger was followed by the correct shaping his body to deliver a right-footed ball with the outside of the boot, produced with such wicked curl and loft it fooled even the great Jaap Stam, falling kindly to Alan Shearer who produced a typically powerful finish past Edwin van der Sar. This game was far from over.

The sea of orange filling three of the four corners in Rotterdam grew louder with to quell the anticipation of a third English goal from the side who topped the scoring charts in terms of team goals in the group stages.

An equaliser soon followed, not from Shearer or Owen or any of the midfield but from a substitute in Martin Keown, replacing an injured Sol Campbell. The Arsenal defender rose highest from a Ryan Giggs corner who, in turn, got his fifth assist of the championships, effectively levelling the sides up with seventeen minutes remaining.

It was, by far and away, the game of the tournament and this particular contest had a lot of life still crammed into it. With McManaman replacing Paul Scholes, Giggs was given the full ninety minutes, or rather, the full hundred and four as the match was taken into extra time—but would not last the distance in the extra time period thanks to the golden goal rule.

David Beckham forced a stupendous save from Van Der Sar thanks to a trademark free-kick whilst Marc Overmars rattled the England post not once but twice either side of the full-time whistle. Then just four minutes from the half-time break in extra time, the Dutch were handed a huge lifeline in their passage to a first major title since 1988.

Edgar Davids jinked through the English line-up, bursting past Martin Keown but was hounded to the ground by Gary Neville, Pierluigi Collina consequently gifted Holland a penalty. A shot from twelve yards to fire themselves through to the semi-finals. Dennis Bergkamp stepped up, standing yards away from several Arsenal teammates but the only one that mattered to him was David Seaman, standing tall in between the sticks rooted to the Dutch soil. The forward placed the ball deep into the left corner. Seaman dived in similar direction, getting a few digits onto the ball and palming it away for the defence to clear.

England were saved. Three minutes later, Ryan Giggs had scored to put them into the semi-finals where world champions France awaited them in Amsterdam.

The Manchester United legend in making had become an overnight English hero, France awaited and a cagey 114 minutes followed. His Arsenal compatriots had stood idly by just over a year ago, watching the winger score one of the greatest FA Cup goals of all-time. This time round they could sit back, relax and drink it in because Giggs rounded the likes of Emmanuel Petit, just like he did at Villa Park in that semi-final but also beating the star-studded, world beating collection of Zidane, Lizarazu, Thuram and Blanc before dribbling the ball through the legs of Fabien Barthez.

Single-handedly Ryan Giggs had pulled England through two knockout rounds against two of the tournament favourites, now England were placed against Italy in the final in Rotterdam. However, England were to be dealt a cruel blow in their European Championship bid before they left the stadium and entered the final, a total of three days were the difference.

The difference, ultimately between success and failure, was dished out by the British media to the ankle ligament damage sustained by the Giggs after the English winger leapfrogged the advertisement hoardings, twisted his ankle dramatically in front of French fans emptying that particular half of the stadium. Giggs would spend the next few hours in hospital, leaving on crutches as English hearts sank, reading the back pages of various newspapers the morning after.

England's best chance at winning a major tournament since the likes of Charlton, Hurst and Moore beat the world in 1966 was dashed thanks to an unnecessary injury to arguably the player of the tournament. Italy would beat them 3-0 in the final and Giggs would collect the player of the tournament award, a simple consolation prize, a poor manufactured replacement for what should have been held up in Rotterdam by Giggs and co.—the Henri Delaunay trophy. Giggs would miss a huge chunk of the 2000-01 season as they were reliant on David Beckham and Dwight Yorke, snatching the Premier League on goal difference from Leeds United.

Giggs scored on his return to football, wrapping up a 5-1 win over Middlesbrough on the penultimate day of the season in May 2001. A summer later, he was becoming instrumental in steering England to World Cup qualification. Ryan Giggs was declared as a forerunner for the Ballon d'Or award in 2000 after losing out in 1999 to Ronaldo but his long-term injury would soon be rewarded with compelling form with the signing of Ruud van Nistelrooy to Manchester

United from PSV Eindhoven.

They had wrapped up the Premier League title and with another Champions League win under his belt in 2002 over Bayer Leverkusen in Glasgow, Giggs was confident, and this time he was in goalscoring form for England throughout the 2002 FIFA World Cup qualifiers he did take part in. Two goals against Finland followed by another brace against Germany was all leading up to the grand finale, Giggs poked home the winner in first half stoppage time against Greece at Old Trafford in a slim 1-0 win which helped England top the group ahead of Germany going into the finals. England were handed the proclaimed 'group of death' once more as the likes of Sweden, Argentina and Nigeria awaited England, but they were co-favourites to win the tournament in the Far East, alongside four-time champions, Brazil.

Due to 'rustiness' Sven-Goran Eriksson left Giggs out of the starting eleven against Sweden in the opener much to the dismay of the English contingent in Japan's Saitama Stadium. After falling a goal behind thanks to Marcus Allback, Eriksson was forced to eat his own words after hauling Trevor Sinclair off the pitch at half-time. Giggs would notch up a goal as England saunter to a routine 4-1 win to stamp themselves on the tournament.

A Shearer-inspired victory against Argentina left England only needing a point against Nigeria to confirm a second round berth against Denmark. Goals from the Manchester United duo of Gary Neville and Paul Scholes would help England record a 3-0 win against the Africans and England hit one better against the Danes, with Giggs getting on the scoresheet twice more.

This left the mighty Brazil, the two co-favourites were meeting in the last eight stage, Giggs was on three goals, Ronaldo topped the scoring charts with five but Michael Owen was also about to announce himself on the tournament. Owen netted against Sweden but would add two more against an adventurous Brazil side who would retaliate with unnerving accuracy and speed as Rivaldo got both goals in a match billed by the half-time pundits, Gary Lineker and Alan Hansen as Rivaldo v. Owen.

Ryan Giggs would have a massive say on the final result too. An innocuous free-kick from Ronaldinho would be charged down by Steven Gerrard, offloaded to David Beckham before the Manchester United winger pinged a diagonal ball to Michael Owen, who instead of gunning for his hat-trick slipped the ball to Ryan Giggs who rolled the ball into an empty net, finishing the match off, leaving England with Turkey as their only remaining obstacle in the semi-final. Germany were the inspiration and the opponents to set-up yet another World Cup final, mirroring 1966.

Turkey were carved up by Ryan Giggs and co. in the semi-final with the winger getting two goals in a demolition job of the fellow Europeans as England cruised into their second World Cup final, winning 4-1 on the night.

This was the night every Englishman had been dreaming about—another World Cup final date with Germany. They both had a couple of men in-form. Giggs and Owen were full of goals whilst Germany housed the competition's top goalscorer with Miroslav Klose on seven. He wouldn't be eclipsed in terms of goals, but Germany weren't about to add to their three World Cup titles, the agony of '66 returned in

Yokohama.

Owen got the early goal in what was a dull final, only brightened up with the inclusion of Michael Ballack who caused England danger in the second half courtesy of a few long distance efforts. It only needed one to sneak under David Seaman for the game to be re-ignited back into life. On the 83rd minute, the aforementioned cruelly happened for the English goalkeeper.

Seaman would announce his international retirement shortly after the tournament but his England career still had some time yet. Forty minutes, maximum. Fortunately for England, they weren't dealt the cruel lot of a penalty shootout, nor was the golden goal needed. That man, Ryan Giggs, in the prime of his footballing career simply won the World Cup for England in the 87th minute. A headed goal, of which were sparse in Ryan Giggs' footballing catalogue, was what concluded the World Cup as a contest in 2002, England had brought home football's greatest prize, a second World Cup after thirty-six years of hurt.

The celebrations in London, Manchester, Birmingham and Newcastle amongst many other cities, towns, villages and streets were the like of which many had never seen before. England had taken the game of football to the world and brought it back. Upon their retirements, the likes of Ryan Giggs, David Beckham, Michael Owen and David Seaman would receive instant knighthoods whilst Steven Gerrard and Paul Scholes had to wait a decade or so before receiving theirs.

Giggs' trophy hunt for England wasn't over yet as the golden generation fulfilled their expectations. Whilst for Manchester United, Giggs would net a total of fourteen Premier League titles, two more Champions League crowns and another handful of domestic honours, there was always another international trophy to add to his CV.

The winger would be dealt the heartbreak of missing a penalty in the Euro 2004 final against Spain before being crowned a world champion at the 2006 tournament after netting four goals and being named in the team of the tournament. England would beat France 2-1 in that particular final and the French were beaten in Giggs' swansong tournament in international football two years later.

He would bow out with an assist in a 2-0 final win over France in Vienna at the European Championships in 2008, the only trophy which eluded him throughout his career. Management would be on the horizon for Sir Ryan Giggs of Cardiff.

8

The Head of God

As mentioned in a previous chapter, Diego Maradona wasn't shy to controversy in his time in the game. This chapter will focus on that goal in the 1986 FIFA World Cup quarter final against England as a turning point, no, not the 'goal of the century' as dubbed by many. No, that handball that preceded it by about four minutes.

1986 was Maradona's year to shine with only that tiny blemish to his career in the quarter final, he went onto pick up his one and only World Cup winner's medal with a 3-2 win over Germany in Mexico City. Maradona netted five, one less than England's own Gary Lineker, and picked up the player of the tournament award.

Despite not notching a single goal four years later in Italy, he was selected in the all-star squad, instrumental as Argentina reached yet another World Cup final against Germany. Fresh off a couple of slender wins and penalty shootout victory, Germany claimed football's ultimate prize with their third World Cup title in what was dubbed one of the worst finals in the tournament's history.

Germany won via a late penalty and Argentina became the first nation not to score in a final, going down 1-0 thanks to Andreas Brehme.

That tournament passed without controversy and so did spells in Europe for the Argentine talisman with Barcelona, Napoli and Sevilla clambering for

Maradona's signature in successive stints. However, after one of the goals of the tournament at the 1994 tournament in America against Greece in the group stages, Maradona was pulled aside for a random drugs test following the next group game against Nigeria.

The eye-popping celebrations from the Argentine would be the last he would muster in an international shirt as he left the tournament disgraced in what was billed as his farewell from international football.

The age old debate still rumbles on between Pele and Maradona as to who is the superior with alternatives sometimes offered up such as Zidane, Ronaldo and more recently Lionel Messi and Cristiano Ronaldo. However, you can't help but ask 'where would Diego Maradona be without his controversy?'

What if Diego Maradona attempted a header in the 51st minute in his World Cup quarter-final in 1986 against England?

The world watched with baited breath, Maradona seemed to hang in the air for an eternity before England goalkeeper, Peter Shilton rose above the diminutive playmaker, catching the ball clean with two hands.

In the searing Mexican heat, both sides played out a dull second half and the subsequent thirty minutes of extra time elapsed with no real highlights or threats on either goal. England and Argentina were both foraying into a penalty shootout, a new experience for such established footballing nations.

Lineker would net the crucial penalty, taking England to the final four of the World Cup for the first time in two decades but were beaten by Spain who would ultimately lose out to Germany. For Argentina and Maradona, the re-building process was to be kick-started for the 1990 tournament in Italy.

Maradona was at the height of his powers and led Napoli to their first ever Serie A title in 1987 before bidding farewell to Italy, but only for a few years. Maradona would be back for the World Cup.

With the Copa America in 1987 rapidly approaching, Diego Maradona was developing some headlines of his own, with a reported 8 million fee placed on his head by Real Madrid. His former employers, Barcelona would not be happy when Maradona reached an agreement on the eve of the second group match against Ecuador in Buenos Aries.

Maradona, with some new found confidence, netted a stunning hat-trick which most of the media in Argentina still rave about to this day. They subsequently qualified for the semi-finals, two goals either side of the half-time mark brushing aside Uruguay. Chile would be waiting in the final.

The final wouldn't go as swimmingly as Maradona would have hoped, he was left on the bench after a late night of partying in Buenos Aries and turned up two hours late for a team briefing reportedly "still high off the effects of the previous night" according to some of the hotel staff.

Carlos Bilardo stuck to his guns and sure enough brought his star man into a lifeless 0-0 game on 72 minutes. Within 47 seconds, Maradona had brought Argentina into the lead with an expertly worked goal, dishing the ball out wide to Claudio Caniggia who clipped to ball back onto Maradona's forehead and the rest is history.

Maradona claimed his first piece of silverware on the international stage with the 1987 Copa America. The World Cup would become an obsession with the

Argentine. The forward holed up in Italy with the remainder of his squad three years later, supposedly five months sober in preparation for the tournament.

He was in-form for his club, Real Madrid who had secured their first La Liga title since the capture of Diego Maradona in the 1989-90 season, and claimed the Copa del Rey final where things got a little heated to say the least against Barcelona.

Maradona, as a former Barcelona player, wasn't going to receive the greatest of welcomes playing for their nemesis in Real Madrid. He would be suspended for the November league game against Barcelona at the Nou Camp where Ronald Koeman got the crucial goal in a 2-1 win.

The Argentine would steal the show in the return fixture in April 1990, rolling the ball through Michael Laudrup's legs and striking the ball with such venom, the Barcelona goalkeeper was stranded, and had to simply admire the 30-yard effort as it crashed against the net, Real would go onto win 3-1, and the league.

In the Copa del Rey final, however, which was played at the Mestalla in Valencia, there was a huge Barcelona contingent in the crowd and prior to kick-off there were anti-Maradona and anti-Argentina chants emanating from their fans. The rivalry had reached fever pitch, Spanish newspapers were written not because of the football but because of the violence on and off the pitch between fans and players alike.

74 arrests were made around the stadium that night and that was only the entrée to the main event. Michael Laudrup fired Barcelona into a 17th minute lead to which Hugo Sanchez cancelled out on the stroke of half-time. The play was fair but the atmosphere white hot between the two sets of

supporters. Maradona was quiet throughout the game due to the sheer animosity thrown at him by the Barca fans.

Jeers, bottles and even a sombrero were items launched towards Maradona when he was taking a second half corner. The Argentine replied by stamping on the sombrero and throwing the bottle back where it came, that warranted him a yellow card from the referee.

From the subsequent corner, evidently pent up with rage, Maradona relinquished the role of corner taker, offering a short option for Sanchez. He brought the ball infield a touch before lashing at the ball with all his might, the post-match press release showing pictures of the forward gushing spit out of his mouth signifying the effort and rage the Argentine felt at that moment.

The shot would arrow into the top corner, Maradona had become a hero with Real's second which would be dubbed 'El Objetivo Furioso' which translates loosely to 'The Furious Goal' and would ultimately settle the Copa del Rey in 1990. The game will forever be remembered for those five minutes, either side of the goal though, but for the wrong reasons.

Maradona breached the advertising hoardings, celebrating sarcastically in front of the Barcelona fans. Only a small wave of security staff was standing in between the fans who once adored Diego Maradona and the man himself.

The likes of Bernd Schuster, Fernando Hierro and Hugo Sanchez would celebrate in the all-white strip to further anger the Barcelona fans who were now charging at the flimsy line of security which somehow held strong to part the aggressors and the celebrating pack of players. Video evidence would later show fans spitting on Maradona with the Argentina simply standing there, laughing in the face of adversity.

The Barcelona staff and players didn't like this with Johan Cruyff going head-to-head with his managerial counterpart in John Toshack on the touchline. Some of the substitutes had to split them up but a Welsh right-hand from Toshack dropped Cruyff to the turf which warranted him a two-month touchline ban.

Maradona was fined a substantial amount and a three match suspension was delivered his way, with Ronald Koeman also being issued a lengthy ban for dragging Maradona back over the advertisement boards. This sparked more unsavoury scenes between the two sets of players.

The referee eventually calmed them down, sending Toshack and Koeman off whilst carding Maradona for his over-zealous celebrations, his second bookable offence. Nonetheless, Maradona won the Battle of Valencia, claiming the Copa del Rey. Maradona would help Real Madrid to six successive La Liga titles, prevailing over Johan Cruyff's Barcelona and even beating them in the 1992 European Cup final with a couple of goals from Maradona himself which would effectively lead Cruyff into Barcelona resignation.

After being suspended for the last section of the season, the Argentine playmaker was in fine shape to tackle the world at the 1990 FIFA World Cup in Italy. Maradona led the sides out to face Cameroon, who were supposed to roll over for the Argentines in the opening game.

A late Roger Milla goal left Argentina and Maradona stunned and in desperate need of two wins from the final two group stages matches if they were to qualify.

Four Maradona goals and two substantial wins over Romania and the Soviet Union later and Argentina had qualified as group winners.

They just avoided their enemy Brazil in what would've been an epic second round showdown on goal difference but were fed South American opposition regardless in the shape of Colombia. Maradona didn't pass up the opportunity of a hat-trick in the second round clash, putting Colombia to the sword in a 4-0 hammering which truly showcased Argentina to the world. With seven goals in effectively three matches, Maradona was headed for superstardom and all the riches that the World Cup would bring him.

Then came England. The heartbreak of the 1986 quarter final wouldn't be revisited on this day, however, as Maradona, who was lurking in a clear offside position, netted a goal late in the second half which would seal Argentina's passage into the semi-final, and consequently spark mass outrage from the England players.

Five minutes were eaten up from the protests from the likes of Paul Gascoigne, Peter Shilton and Gary Lineker but the decision would not be reversed as Argentina prevailed and England eliminated.

Maradona would score a penalty in the semi-final shootout against Germany which left Italy in the final. Maradona had taken all the plaudits at the tournament alongside the player of the tournament and golden boot which were waiting for him no matter what the outcome against the hosts was.

Rome was the stage and Argentina simply wiped the floor with the hosts who had a very keen defensive plan in place. They remained stubborn in the first half but would be broken again and again in the second half by Diego Maradona as Italy whimpered to a 3-0 final loss on their own turf, Maradona tearing them apart with a goal and two assists.

Whilst he didn't compete due to a phantom injury at the 1991 Copa America for which he received little to no criticism for as Argentina laboured to a final defeat to Uruguay, he would return to the big leagues at the 1994 FIFA World Cup in America. Maradona was fresh off his second triumph in the Champions League where he scored a first half penalty for Real Madrid in a 2-1 win over AC Milan.

Maradona already stated that he would be ending his professional footballing career for both club and country at the World Cup in the States. He had already bowed out of Real Madrid in successful fashion but Argentina took their time in emulating their 1990 success.

A goalless draw against a poor Greece side followed by an uninspiring 1-0 win over Nigeria, Maradona had failed to register a goal in the opening two games which was a far cry from his nine-goal haul at the previous tournament.

With a win needed for certain qualification against Bulgaria, Maradona stepped up when it mattered most, netting twice in a routine but an unimpressive outing for the Argentines, a 2-1 win. They placed first and were thrown right into the mixer against 1990 final opponents Italy in the second round stage of the tournament.

Maradona and the Argentines looked flat and lifeless in the Foxboro stadium for the Italy tie, a stark contrast from the final four years ago. The comparisons were always going to rain down on a poor Argentine outfit but just when they needed it the most, Maradona rattled his third of the tournament into the net in extra time leaving a path paved by Spain and Germany en route to a final which didn't look likely to compete in.

Diego Maradona was clearly reaching the end of his career but what had changed from the previous month where he scored in a Champions League final victory for his club? Fast forward fifty-odd nights and Maradona was looking stodgy and uninspiring but one thing he could re-locate was his goalscoring touch.

There were reports Maradona was getting his kicks in a different way to football throughout the tournament. Whilst pictures continued to be published about the party-going Maradona, rumours circulated by one of his closest friends and Real Madrid team mate, Hugo Sanchez was that the famous Argentine World Cup winning captain was on a combination of performance-enhancing drugs.

However, the hangovers and the come-downs from the parties and 'medication' were taking a toll on the Argentine's game. After scoring twice in the quarter final against Spain, Maradona was pictured leaving a nightclub in New York in celebration mode, and once more on the eve of the semi-final match in East Rutherford against Germany.

Still, Alfio Basile kept faith in his star man and captain. He would score a penalty in the shootout after a 0-0 draw in the Giants Stadium as Argentina progressed to their second successive final, to face the mighty Brazil.

Tragedy would hit the Argentine side as their captain would be whisked away for a random drugs test following proceedings in New Jersey. Ephedrine along with a couple of unnamed class-A drugs were found in the footballer's system. He was effectively suspended for the rest of the tournament and hit with a ten-month suspension from all forms of the game. Maradona would pick up his coaching career the following May.

However, he would have to cheer on his compatriots from deep inside the executive seating area in the Rose Bowl in Pasadena. Argentina would win via another penalty shootout to claim their third World Cup, drawing them level on titles with Brazil in a bizarre tournament for the Argentines. Many claimed they didn't deserve the tournament for the way their captain behaved and was consequently suspended or even because of the under-par class of football showcased at the finals by the side.

Whichever way you looked at it, within the space of twenty-four months, Maradona was celebrating another UEFA Champions League medal. This one, however, would be one as manager of Real Madrid, led by the frontline of Gabriel Batistuta and Ronaldo. Five La Liga titles would be won with the exception of the 1999-2000 title which went the way of Valencia but Maradona would claim three Copa del Rey crowns as well as two successive Champions League titles in 1998 and 1999.

He would retire from all forms of the game in 2001 after a fourth managerial Champions League victory over Leeds United in a 3-1 win in the San Siro, Ronaldo scoring a perfect hat-trick. A fitting way to cap off one of the greatest careers in football history.

9

Akinbiyi, Goal Machine

Ade Akinbiyi was a journeyman of sorts when it came to his latter days as a professional footballer. He did make a couple of high profile moves in England, the biggest of which came in 2000 as he switched to Leicester City from Wolverhampton Wanderers, acting as a replacement for Emile Heskey.

5.5 million was the fee and it was a big money move for Akinbiyi who was allowed just ten months at Wolves as they attempted to atone for Robbie Keane's move to Coventry City. All of this came purely out of the free-scoring talent that everybody witnessed throughout his days at Gillingham and Bristol City as he netted 21 in a single season for the latter outfit.

Akinbiyi became a cult figure in English football in the 2000-01 season when he went eight months without scoring a single goal in a blue shirt after promising start in the Premier League. The decline from what was a strong, tough and free-scoring Nigerian forward was rapid, his confidence was shot consistently by Leicester boss Dave Bassett who labelled him an "average striker" after a match with Liverpool.

When he did break the long, fifteen match goal drought in November 2001, he almost tore the shirt from his back in the 1-0 win at home to Sunderland in the league. Leicester would be relegated that season, Akinbiyi escaped Filbert Street for a whopping 2.2

million fee for Crystal Palace prior to the demotion to the First Division though.

Thirteen goals in sixty-seven appearances wasn't the best return for a player supposedly meant to replace one of England's best strikers of the time in Heskey. In a similar period at Palace he scored three times before a short stint at Stoke City.

He would complete a 600,000 pound move to Burnley in February 2005 and two minutes into his debut was sent off for a headbutt against Sunderland, he would be sold to Sheffield United eleven months later. He'd score seventeen times in the next three years which featured a stint with the Blades and a second outing at Burnley before he scored once in twenty-nine appearances for Houston Dynamo and Notts County towards the end of his career.

As a youngster, Akinbiyi looked for the entire world to be a natural-born goalscorer in his days at Bristol City but his potential wasn't fulfilled.

Going back to his Leicester City spell, what if Ade Akinbiyi kept up his form and turned into one of the biggest prospects in the Premier League?

After transferring for 5.5 million in pre-season to replace Emile Heskey, Peter Taylor announced Akinbiyi as a player for the future, claiming that he'd be a big part of the Premier League in the not too distant future.

Akinbiyi proved Taylor right in the opening month, scoring six goals in the opening four matches he was named as the season's opening player of the month as Leicester City occupied third position and even defeated champions, Manchester United at Old Trafford thanks to a brace from the Nigerian forward.

Leicester would finish sixth place in the Premier

League, pipping Chelsea to a European spot on the last day. Akinbiyi scored 24 goals in all competitions, remaining Leicester's top goalscorer throughout the season. The Foxes didn't do too badly in Europe either. Thanks to Akinbiyi's two goals over the two legs, Leicester progressed past Red Star Belgrade in the first round before beating the likes of Celta Vigo, Shakhtar Donetsk and Stuttgart as they reached a quarter final tie with the mighty Barcelona.

A heroic 1-0 win at Filbert Street thanks to a late winner from the man himself, Akinbiyi wasn't enough over the course of the two legs as a Patrick Kluivert masterclass at the Nou Camp helped Barcelona to a 6-1 aggregate victory. Liverpool would win the tournament with a win over Alaves but Akinbiyi and Leicester were left proud of their achievements for the season.

Martin O'Neill quickly returned to Filbert Street after a season-long spell in charge of Celtic, promising the best period in the history of the club after a pre-season friendly win over Inter Milan in July 2001.

O'Neill sniffed out such deals as signing the duo of Ruud van Nistelrooy and Robert Pires after the latter had an abysmal first season at Arsenal. Leicester had new found wealth from an amazing run over the past couple of years and O'Neill wasn't frightened to spend it on big names.

Akinbiyi didn't take a back seat because of van Nistelrooy's signing, however, the Nigerian would complete another season as Leicester's top goalscorer, scoring 39 times in 58 appearances for the club, with the new Dutch influx only managing 21. Leicester would make the UEFA Cup final and, amazingly, not relinquish a good league position as they battled to third position, beating Newcastle United to the final Champions League position. Akinbiyi netted eleven goals in an amazing UEFA Cup run, scoring twice in the final against Roma in the final although it would ultimately end in penalty shootout heartbreak for the Nigerian who had a World Cup to prepare for in the far east.

Being in the same company as England, Sweden and Argentina was always going to be difficult and they were eliminated at the group stages. Akinbiyi's two goals against Argentina sank one of the pre-tournament favourites but would be beaten by Sweden and held to a draw by England as Akinbiyi picked up four goals in the three group stage matches he played in.

Coming off the back of a pretty successful World Cup for Akinbiyi, he darted his eyes across Europe, ingesting the interest across the continent for the free-scoring forward. Barcelona attempted to buy the Leicester talisman for 17 million but Leicester rejected this and higher offers from the likes of Arsenal, Borussia Dortmund and Juventus.

The signings of such players as Tomas Rosicky and Dimitar Berbatov from German clubs Dortmund and Leverkusen respectively didn't entice Akinbiyi into another term at Leicester as he left on the eve of the club's start to the Premier League season.

The Nigerian's goals would entice a certain Sir Alex Ferguson to sign the forward after missing out on Ruud van Nistelrooy the previous season. United were out to re-claim the Premier League trophy back from Arsenal after finishing second in the previous season.

Fast forward four months down the line and United were placed eighth in the Premier League after a horrendous start to the season which featured no league goals for Ade Akinbiyi after 14 league matches and two dismissals in a tumultuous period for the Nigerian.

The only goal Akinbiyi notched was in the opening Champions League group stage match against Maccabi Haifi where United were already 5-2 ahead at Old Trafford. The Nigerian needed settling into a big club with huge expectations in comparison to Leicester City. Nonetheless, Fergie sold him in January at a discounted price of eight million (a fraction of the twenty-two that United had paid for him five months previously) to Spanish giants Real Madrid.

Another five months later Akinbiyi was picking up his first piece of silverware as Real Madrid sauntered to the 2002-03 La Liga title, pipping Deportivo to the league crown by some fourteen points. The Nigerian was in some good company, partnering Ronaldo up front for the Galacticos who also had the likes of Zidane, Figo and Casillas in their ranks.

He hit seven goals in ten appearances in his first half-season at the club and was promised more football, even when Real added former teammate David Beckham to their star-studded line-up.

In fact, by the following Easter, Akinbiyi was keeping Ronaldo out of the squad with his thirty-some goals in almost as many appearances. A night that will live long in the memory for the Nigerian came in a Champions League quarter final in April 2004 where his two goals sank former club, Manchester United.

Akinbiyi would get a further six goals in the term as Real Madrid faltered at the semi-final stage of both the Champions League and the Copa del Rey but would retain their La Liga title in similar fashion to the previous season. Akinbiyi was a Galactico.

A third La Liga crown as well as his 75th goal in the all-white of Real Madrid would be the milestones reached in the 2004-05 season for Akinbiyi, a far cry from playing in the crumbling stadium of Filbert Street which was his footballing home some three years previously. The icing on top of the cake for the Nigerian was his first European title coming in the May of 2005.

As a former United player he didn't receive the best welcome in Istanbul against Liverpool in the final of the Champions League but he would get the decisive goal in a dull 1-0 win for Real as they snatched the 10th crown away from Liverpool who were gunning for their fifth. Akinbiyi continued in similar fashion the following season, winning a successive Champions League and La Liga double but also netting a hat-trick in the Copa del Rey final against Espanyol.

Akinbiyi had officially arrived on the world stage and what better than a treble for club to prepare you for the 2006 FIFA World Cup. A group containing the likes of Iran, Mexico and Portugal was never going to be an easy week in Nigerian football. Four goals for Akinbiyi left Nigeria in second place behind Portugal on six points as the Nigerian entered the second round clash against Holland as the tournament's top scorer.

He was up against former team mate and opponent Ruud van Nistelrooy who didn't have the best friendship at Leicester and the Dutch international was still there, scoring the goals to keep them in the division as they had crumbled following Akinbiyi's departure.

An early yellow card for Ruud was meant to unnerve Akinbiyi as the Dutch attempted to get under the 2005

Ballon d'Or winner's skin. It wasn't to be. The Nigerian maestro netted very late on in extra time to progress the nation to their first World Cup quarter final.

The goal in the second round put Akinbiyi on thirty-seven goals and at what was most likely to be his final World Cup, he wanted to surpass Rashidi Yekini's national goalscoring record in the quarter final against England. Most of his old opponents stood in the way of a historic first African nation in the final four of the World Cup.

Akinbiyi netted his sixth tournament goal early on to put Nigeria in the driving seat but after an unnecessary two-footed lunge on Steven Gerrard, Akinbiyi was dismissed in the second half, leaving England to run riot in his absence, scoring twice in the final fifteen minutes of the game. England would bow out in the following round whilst Akinbiyi was banned for a year by his nation for his behaviour at the tournament despite collecting the tournament's Golden Boot and being the nation's top goalscorer.

He fled back to the Bernabeu a disgraced name in Nigerian football and would never play again for the national side. For the Nigerian, a further La Liga title was in store but he would be driven out of the club due to numerous racial incidents towards the tail-end of the season from opposition fans.

Akinbiyi handed in a transfer request and was sold at the end of the 2006-07 season to Chelsea where he played out the remainder of his career, retiring in 2011 with an FA Cup and a Premier League to his name. He would enter the Nigerian football hall of fame after a lot of deliberation in 2016 and had his name solidified in the record books for both club and country as one of the game's greats.

10

Ray Wilkins, FIFA President

Nowadays Ray Wilkins plies his trade as a pundit for *Sky Sports* of a weekend and during Champions League broadcasts on a weekday. Wilkins is best known for starting his career with stints at Chelsea and Manchester United which fired him into the England team where he garnered a very respectable 84 caps.

Whilst many know him as the bald man by the side of a slew of Chelsea managers in the dugout as a coach, assistant manager and caretaker manager, he could play a bit of football himself once upon a time.

He did gain infamy as he became the first England player to be sent off for innocuously throwing a ball at the referee in the group stage match against Morocco at the 1986 FIFA World Cup which would effectively rule him out for the remainder of the tournament after not being selected for the vital quarter final against Argentina.

Wilkins made his final appearance in an England shirt in November of that year before retiring from the international squad. He captained England ten times and remains 13th on the all-time appearances list for England, at the time of writing.

Stints abroad for clubs such as A.C. Milan and Paris Saint-Germain prolonged Wilkins' career before a two-year period at Rangers. He would settle, largely, south of the border at clubs such as Crystal Palace and Queens Park Rangers, the latter of which he spent the time as the player-manager.

Whilst a Chelsea boy at heart, he will be remembered by most of the clubs he put a shift in for down the years. His commentary might not be up to scratch but Carlo Ancelotti dished out a huge commendation in his autobiography, stating that they wouldn't have won a thing without him.

With the accusations landing on the head of Sepp Blatter in the past couple of years because of suspected bribery in the build-up to the bids for the FIFA World Cups for the 2018 and 2022 tournaments which was concluded in December 2010. In some bizarre alternate universe, what would happen if Ray Wilkins rose up the FIFA dignitary ladder?

Ray Wilkins announces himself as a candidate for FIFA President for the elections in August 2014.

After the affairs with the FIFA World Cup bids, nobody wished to put themselves forward as a candidate for the FIFA presidential election which took place just a month after Spain's second successive World Cup title was won in Rio de Janeiro.

Wilkins could be seen attending almost all of the evening matches at the World Cup in Brazil, rubbing shoulders with the outgoing president in Sepp Blatter who was found guilty of accepting bribes for the World Cup bids in 2010.

The former England international would win the presidential election at FIFA, as the votes were tallied at the FIFA Congress in Budapest on August 14th, 2014 where Wilkins won the right to become the FIFA President with no apparent opposition.

After Blatter and Platini's collaboration of anti-technology ideologies, Wilkins successfully green lit plans for goal line technology at the forthcoming

Confederations Cup and FIFA World Cup tournaments which left Platini to follow suit for all UEFA competitions.

By 2016, technology was in place in the top four divisions of English football and in 27 of Europe's top flight divisions, and ten second-tier European divisions. The European Championships were a success in terms of the sparkling new technology as a Poland goal which possibly wouldn't have been seen by the officials was challenged by the players and would be allowed. This granted Poland a place in the knockout stages of the tournament.

Wilkins was consistently receiving praise for revolutionising and modernising the game of football. Football had finally caught up with its counterparts with its technology ruling. However, by the 2018 FIFA World Cup, Ray Wilkins wasn't that loved in the world of football.

The former Chelsea assistant had "driven the game into disrepute" according to Michel Platini who made a damning account of Wilkins upon his resignation as UEFA president in the summer of 2017.

To make room on the television schedule for further football programming, Wilkins reduced the time of matches to two thirty-minute halves which in turn registered a massive profit for the likes of *Sky Sports* and ITV who took in almost double of their revenue. 8 Premier League games a weekend would be shown whilst all cup matches were televised live, distributed by different stations.

If many in the media were outraged by Wilkins' latest ruling, then the next would shock all of football. Wilkins declared that substitutions would no longer be allowed as the maximum allowed pitch size was seventy by forty yards as teams could now only select eight players for a match.

These extraordinary rules, which were being dubbed as "revolutionary rules" by Wilkins himself, were capped off by an increase in goal size by 35% in an industry-wide ruling in July 2019.

3,000 goals were seen in the Premier League for the 2019/20 season as Daniel Sturridge scored 67 goals in the season, a record as games would more often reach double figures due to the sheer size of the goals. The European Championships in 2020 was the highest scoring in history as France went onto beat Portugal in the final, victorious in an incredible 9-7 win.

The sport in general was being labelled a farce as Time magazine even did a feature-length article on the FIFA President, who they claimed was "destroying the sport's enjoyment". Whilst the nation's media was now becoming consistent in their ruing of the Wilkins presidential appointment, the participation in the sport had reportedly increased by 20% in Britain, with similar increases across Europe.

North America recorded a 35% increase in junior participation which led to it overtaking Ice Hockey and even Baseball in terms of popularity. United States rose in the FIFA rankings to third and were becoming one of the world's footballing powerhouses.

By the time the 2022 World Cup swung around, which was moved to be hosted in the States, they were one of the bookmaker's favourites to the win the tournament. There was still time for more ludicrous rules to be sanctioned by the FIFA President though.

The media, who were now in tune with the absurdity behind Wilkins' presidential mind, called for more rules to adapt the "New Era" phase of football which had been coined by former president Sepp Blatter. Blatter claimed, in an interview with The Guardian in November 2021 that Wilkins had left the game "inoperable and damaged beyond repair courtesy of the outrageous English brain of his".

Whilst there was increasingly becoming no love lost between England and the notoriously neutral Switzerland, Wilkins would go ahead with plans to abolish the offside rule in time for the 2022 FIFA World Cup.

Again, the industry-wide ruling was recognised by UEFA but not before he could disturb one of the rules that he hadn't gone anywhere near touching since his election seven years previously, seven years in which he had transformed the game.

Wilkins announced from a FIFA congress in Sion, Switzerland—where he faced a protest outside the building prior to the announcement—that the points system both in tournaments and in league format would be changed for the foreseeable future.

Four points would be collected for a win by four clear goals and score draws above 4-4 would warrant two points for both sides whilst an increasingly unlikely goalless draw would warrant a -2 point deduction for both teams.

Power-mad was a word becoming synonymous with Wilkins as he oversaw the highest-scoring FIFA World Cup in history as Chile would win their first ever title, beating outsiders Russia 15-12 in the final. The rugby scores were becoming genuine football scores.

For the first time in World Cup history, a nation qualified from the group stages with more than nine points as Spain recorded five-goal deficit wins over the likes of Montenegro and Gabon and thus qualifying with eleven points from three games.

The Premier League in 2023 would be won by a total of 102 points—another record, and from thirty wins, a mathematical impossibility in the past, but not under Wilkins' tenure. The impossible was becoming possible.

Prior to the 2024 European Championships, which Wilkins somehow managed to bring to England amidst a lot of controversy considering favouritism, he passed the '3-goal defender' law which ensured that every goal scored by a registered defender counting for three goals. This above most laws changed the entire tactics in the sport within teams as most managers would field defenders up front to gain an advantage.

The most famous exploitation of this law would come into effect in the final of the European Championships as England made their first final since 1966 and two Gary Cahill goals accumulated six goals for England who would beat Italy 8-5, in a low-scoring affair for the new era of football.

One final rule would be the death of Ray Wilkins as president of FIFA on the day of his tenth anniversary. He passed a law which suspended the use of a goalkeeper's arms alongside a multi-ball rule in the last five minutes of the match. The Premier League's opening weekend would be the test subject for these new rules and the opening weekend of games consisted of 264 goals, the highest scoring of which saw Cardiff surprising Chelsea 24-20, picking up four points to lead the table after the first match.

Wilkins would be ushered out by an almost unanimous vote at the 2024 presidential election in December which would be won by former UEFA president in Michel Platini. The Frenchman's first act was to rescind all of the laws which Wilkins helped pass and, believe it or not, the first Premier League game under Platini's presidential tenure, with the more traditional rules in place, ended 0-0 between Everton and Southampton.

Platini would restore the beautiful game back to its normal rules, with the only exception being goal line technology which would remain in place. For Wilkins, however, his reputation was tarnished and would see out his days in hiding after a tumultuous reign as FIFA President, the like of which we have never seen, or will see ever again.

11

Bald Baggio

If you were to select an all-time greatest eleven for the Italian national team, Roberto Baggio wouldn't stray too far from the list. He might face stiff opposition from Paolo Rossi and Alessandro del Piero but Italians can safely agree that he was their star man in the 1994 FIFA World Cup.

The man the media liked to call "The Divine Ponytail" had appeared at Italia 90 but played a bit part in ensuring Italy placed third in the tournament, scoring the odd goal throughout the tournament. Four years on, however, Baggio rescued a faltering Italian World Cup bid in America after floundering to a loss over Ireland. Italy would rack up four points in the group stage and finish as one of the best third placed sides in the tournament, progressing to the knockout stage.

He was sacrificed in the 1-0 win over Norway in the group stage thanks to their goalkeeper receiving a red card so he wasn't able to lead Italy to a win at the tournament until the second round.

This is where he came alive. After looking down and out against Nigeria, Baggio netted his first of the tournament two minutes from time before adding a winning penalty in the first period of extra time. Another goal in the 88th minute in the quarter final wrapped up the tie against Spain as he got another winning goal to squeeze Italy through to the final four.

Two more goals against German conquerors, Bulgaria

solidified Baggio's reputation in Italy as his first half quick-fire double set Italy on their way for a chance at surpassing Brazil's record of three World Cup crowns. In a dull final against Brazil, it came down to the lottery of a penalty shootout, where Baggio was registered to take Italy's fifth and final penalty. It would be the final kick of the tournament. The Italian drilled the ball, missing the target, just like Diana Ross in the opening ceremony a month previously, and subsequently sent the ball and Italy's hopes of a World Cup into orbit.

He would score two crucial goals in a more impressive 1998 group stage showing at the World Cup hosted in France four years later. He would be dropped for the second round win over Norway before coming on to exorcise some demons by netting in a penalty shootout in the quarter final against the hosts, France in another penalty disaster for the Italians.

Baggio is one of football's wasted potentials. After the 1998 World Cup, where Del Piero was largely preferred when fit, he would never grace the world stage ever again. He would remain in Italy, claiming that he needed to stay in the country in order to get into Giovanni Trapattoni's 2002 squad for the World Cup in the Far East, which he couldn't achieve.

After spending two years each at both Milan clubs as well as a successful stint at Juventus earlier in his career, Baggio fizzled out into obscurity with a decent goal return at Brescia, plumping to remain in Serie A until he retired in 2004.

Could "Il Divin' Codino" have seen off the South Koreans in the World Cup in 2002 or helped Italy over the line in the Euro 2000 final against France?

Crawling through the honours that Baggio won for his club is quick and simple, it reads just two successive Serie A crowns in 1995 and 1996, with a Coppa Italia and UEFA Cup winners medal with Juventus. This was followed by a UEFA Intertoto Cup medal with Bologna in 1998.

However, the runners-up medals are a long list, defining Baggio as a "nearly man", losing out on two UEFA Cups in the early nineties, reaching the final of four Coppa Italias, but winning only one and above all else, only winning the Silver Ball (tournament's second best player) at the 1994 FIFA World Cup. The award for the best player went to Romario, who lifted the trophy, which could have been Baggio's fate had he netted that crucial penalty in the final against Brazil.

What if Roberto Baggio shaved his hair off, starting his career at Vicenza ponytail-less, and leaving himself short up top throughout his footballing life?

Baggio was announced as Fiorentina's new signing in 1984 after a couple of years at Vicenza where he helped them to promotion to Serie B in 1983. After placing fourth in the second tier of Italian football with thirty-two goals to his name, Fiorentina were quick to snap up the young home-grown Italian playmaker.

At 17 years of age, nothing big was expected of Baggio at Fiorentina in the 1984-85 season. In an innocuous Coppa Italia match against Empoli, in the fourth round, Baggio debuted. Ninety minutes later The Viola's fans were singing his name after his four goals secured a 5-0 cup win.

He would go onto score ten times in twenty-nine games in the remainder of a season, the Italian teenager had all but secured a place in the starting eleven in Florence. After placing seventh in the league,

Baggio and Fiorentina narrowly missed out on European football.

Baggio was becoming a sensation in the Tuscany region; he went onto lift the Coppa Italia in 1986 with Fiorentina, with a highlight in the season coming in a 4-2 win over Torino where he single-handedly won them the match, netting a hat-trick.

However, the highlight of the season for the man they call Roberto came in the off-season, two days after receiving his first chunk of silverware. Enzo Bearzot, the man who brought a third World Cup to Italy at the previous tournament called up the youngster to the national side for what would have been his first cap.

Italy crashed out at the second round stage to France and Baggio went unused throughout the tournament. The experience was vital though. A run in the Cup Winners' Cup gained Baggio determination in the 1986-87 season as he scored eight goals as Fiorentina fell at the final four hurdle, losing out to Bordeaux despite three goals in the tie from Baggio in a 7-4 aggregate defeat.

Baggio was definitely the talk of the town and he won his first international appearance shortly after the failure of the 1986 World Cup. He would represent the national side at the Euro 88 tournament, scoring just one goal in the tournament as Italy were dumped out at the group stages.

Meanwhile in Florence, Baggio was kicking up a big fuss, even fees in their millions were being thrown about in the tabloids with teams such as Juventus, Real Madrid and Liverpool heading the interest.

However, Roberto wasn't going to be swayed, netting another twenty-seven goals in the 1988-89 Serie A campaign which went some way to winning

Fiorentina their third Serie A crown, plucking the title away from Juve on the final day with a 3-2 win over A.C. Milan.

Baggio declared that he would stay in Italy until they hosted the World Cup in 1990 and he surpassed his own expectation. Another Serie A followed as well as that illusive UEFA Cup crown, beating Werder Bremen 3-2 on aggregate in the 1990 final. The shaved head of Baggio's was becoming national fashion as he helped Italy to their first tournament semi-final since 1982, scoring four goals on the way and helping Italy over the line against West Germany in the quarter finals.

He would remain in Italy for another few years, finally caving into the interest of Juventus, for a fee of 4 million. Two more Serie A crowns awaited Baggio up until his departure in 1993 with only the European Cup escaping him in the 1992 final.

After scoring in every round for Juventus, including a hat-trick against Kaiserslautern in the first round, Baggio would net four in the group stages, as Juventus sailed through a group containing Anderlecht, Panathinaikos and Dynamo Kiev to book their final destiny.

Barcelona were the opponents at Wembley and an early goal from Salvatore Schillaci put the Italians in front. However, goals from Michael Laudrup and Hristo Stoichkov helped Barcelona to a second half 2-1 lead in the English capital. Some argue to this day whether or not Casiraghi dived in second half stoppage time to win a last-gasp penalty.

Whilst there has been disagreement down the years about the awarding the penalty, everybody in Italy can agree that Baggio should not have taken the cocky approach to the penalty. Italian teammate and

Sampdoria forward at the time, Gianluca Vialli said in an interview days later; "When you score twenty or more goals a season for a team like Juventus and win all of these prizes and tournaments, you become immortal, Baggio was that the other night. You could see the confidence coming out of him, and see it drain when he chipped the ball over the crossbar. Any forward would tell you to try and burst the net in that situation, but no, Baggio is a different class of player."

The subsequent European Championships in 1992, were a unmitigated disaster. No goals and a red card for Baggio left Italy spiralling out of the group stages after the second match. Just four goals in twenty-one appearances for his club the following season left Juventus trophyless and Baggio destined elsewhere.

Baggio became a recluse in the final year in Italy before finally deciding to move away from his home country after fearing for his safety after the Juventus fans who once adored him were now labelling him a villain.

After the twelve months that Baggio had endured there weren't as many takers for the Italian's signature. However, the free-spending Jack Walker came in with an eight million pound bid which rippled throughout Italy. Could the prodigal son be shipped out to distant shores?

The answer: almost immediately. Baggio didn't even do as much as wave goodbye to Turin, he hopped on one of the first flights to the north-west of England where he would ply his trade at the less-than-sunny climate of Blackburn.

An opening day hat-trick for Baggio against Aston Villa settled any doubters prior to the match. Baggio claimed that he could out-score the rest of the division's forwards in the season, stating that it would be a warm-up for the main event in the summer—the 1994 World Cup.

Thirty-one league goals and an FA Cup runners-up medal later, Baggio had become immortalised at the Lancashire club and he followed through on his promise, topping the scoring charts ahead of Eric Cantona and teammate, Alan Shearer. The combination with Shearer was lapping up praise all around Europe, but the league title had eluded them by a couple of points from Manchester United.

Baggio was back in the good books of Italian boss Arrigo Sacchi just in time for the World Cup in America. Italy steamrolled through the group containing Ireland, Norway and Mexico, scoring five times in the group, which included a hat-trick against Norway in a 5-0 win and a double over Mexico.

They recorded maximum points but two yellow cards in the opening three matches for Baggio meant Italy would miss their rejuvenated star man for the second round clash against Nigeria. Italy won on penalties after a meagre 0-0 draw but just days later, Baggio would clinch a brace in the 2-0 quarter-final win over Spain.

Germany gained a semi-final berth thanks to a slim win over underdogs Bulgaria but it looked as though Italy's run was coming to an end as the half-time whistle was sounded. Another Baggio penalty miss looked to have brought back memories of the 1992 European Cup final but even after a Jurgen Klinsmann opener, Baggio would retaliate with an equaliser and consequently send the game into penalties. The bald assassin, as he was named in Lancashire, scored his first penalty in three years in the shootout as Italy progressed to meet Brazil in the final in California.

The stage was set for a superb outing from both nations; whoever won the match would pick up their fourth World Cup crown. After a stale 89 minutes, a poor cross from the right evaded everybody but defender Dunga, only for his wayward clearance to ricochet off Baggio's knee to find its path diverted towards the top corner. Italy were the unlikely winners, Baggio the likely hero as they celebrated their fourth crown well into the night.

Retrospectively, Baggio claims that this was the highlight of his career, the greatest goal he ever scored even despite the luck factored into it. Blackburn's free-spending power brought the pairing of Rivaldo and Zinedine Zidane after much deliberation by Jack Walker in the summer whether or not to keep Tim Sherwood.

The pressure in the side to compete for all the domestic honours, despite all of the glory that Baggio had achieved over the summer, was enough to divert the automatic success that the media had predicted. The three had all gone their separate ways by 1997 as Baggio left Blackburn the previous year after his tenure in Lancashire which generated no trophies.

The Italian playmaker was soon shipped off to London where he would turn out for his debut in the claret and blue of West Ham in their final Premier League match of the 1996-97 season, scoring twice to keep them up with a win over Chelsea. After such a brilliant display, West Ham fans were purring at the prospect of Baggio for the upcoming 1997-98 season. However, despite scoring at home to Barnsley in a 3-0 opening day victory, Baggio would have to be carried on a stretcher in an afternoon which Baggio has since declared as his worst outing on a football pitch.

A fifty-fifty challenge, dished the ball out elsewhere and the clattering of two onrushing footballing talent left Baggio with a double fracture and an open dislocation of his left fibula bone, in layman's terms: a broken leg.

It would effectively end Baggio's stint in the top flight of any European football league as two years later he announced his return to the game for Nottingham Forest for the start of the 1999-2000 season in the second tier of English football, costing the club only 400,000.

After declaring himself fit, he didn't make his debut at Forest until January when he scored four times against non-league Stevenage Borough in an FA Cup third round tie. He wouldn't be dropped for another game as Forest marginally missed out on the play-offs despite Baggio's excellent return of 19 goals from 17 matches and an unbeaten run of twelve matches in the final portion of the season.

Baggio stated in a pre-season interview in August 2000 with BBC's *Football Focus* that he wanted to end his career at Forest, because of the club's history. The fans were delighted with this show of strength, particularly after Tottenham Hotspur's attempts to sign the playmaker throughout the summer.

The Italian would take Forest back to the play-offs, scoring twenty-four times as the Nottinghamshire club were dumped out at the semi-final stage by Birmingham City. Two more seasons would pass and Baggio was still committed to the cause as Forest were left with back-to-back play-off final heartbreaks against Birmingham again in 2002 and Wolverhampton Wanderers to round off the 2002-03 season.

Just when he was about to give up any hope on Forest in 2004, they earned sixth place on the final day thanks to a 2-1 win with Crystal Palace who were also vying for that position as Forest secured their play-off position once more. Baggio scored twice in a 3-0 away win over Sunderland in the subsequent play-off semifinal which left the 3-1 second leg defeat at home redundant.

Baggio was making his third successive play-off final appearance, a record, which wouldn't be extended by the Italian. The final day etched into the English footballing calendar was the play-off final between Nottingham Forest and Ipswich Town. For Baggio, he could finally reach the pinnacle of the Premier League and this time he would be able to enjoy it.

An early goal from Ipswich didn't deter the Italian as he scored twice in the second half. The celebrations were almost spilling out onto the pitch as the fans, who had waited since their Premier League relegation in 1999 for this, were ready to invade the Millennium Stadium turf.

A long ball from a Forest defender in the final ebb of the match found Baggio in behind the defence, with room to spare. As the Italian collected the ball and spun on it, he had acres of room to run into. Two choices laid out in front of him: a) kill the game off with a third goal, b) run down the remainder of second half injury time in the corner.

A third choice only became apparently when Baggio spun on a sixpence. That choice wasn't made clear to the public until the following day. Baggio limped up to collect his medals with the pundits none the wiser about the injury which would effectively retire the

Italian and cruelly steal the twilight of his career in the Premier League away from him.

As Baggio turned he ruptured his cruciate knee ligaments and, at the age of 37, he was forced to hang up his boots. He declared his retirement from football in June 2004. Forest would be immediately relegated from the top flight, amassing seventeen points in a disparaging stay in the top division. Three years later they would find themselves in the third tier of English football before promotion back up to the Championship in 2011.

Forest were restored to what they were prior to Baggio's transfer but for the Italian there will always be what ifs hanging above his head.

12

Seeing Red

Roy Keane is one of the all-time greats at Manchester United; he has won it all besides the UEFA Champions League which eluded him thanks to suspension for the 1999 final against Bayern Munich. He captained the club to the greatest season United have ever had in terms of success as they won the unprecedented Treble which consisted of the Champions League, the FA Cup and the Premier League crown which were all wrapped up within ten history-making days in May 1999.

However, prior to that historic season, Keane spent a large chunk of the 1997-98 season out with an anterior knee ligament injury, caused by a certain Alf-Inge Haaland of Leeds United. The Norwegian apparently criticised Roy Keane for a foul during the league encounter in September 1997 and claimed that he was feigning to avoid punishment.

Keane was cautioned by the referee in the match and he made his long-awaiting return from injury to football, playing in the Charity Shield match at Wembley against Arsenal in August 1998. Keano, as he is known around Old Trafford, would complete the next three seasons with successive Premier League titles, adding to the previous four he had accumulated at the club.

However, in the Manchester derby in late April 2001, almost four years after the incident at Elland Road where he injured his knee ligaments, Roy Keane exacted his revenge on the now-Manchester City player. A deliberate knee-high studded challenge on Alf-Inge Haaland effectively ended the Norwegian's career as he didn't complete a full match again, finally retiring in 2003 after failed recovery attempts from the injury sustained by Keane's tackle.

The Manchester United captain would serve an initial three-game suspension and a small fine as United picked up another title along the way but another year passed and the story resurfaced upon the publication of *Keane*, the Manchester United captain's autobiography.

In the autobiography which was published in August 2002, Keane states how the tackle was a premeditated attack on the City player for his criticism in the 1997 clash with Leeds United. For this remark and several other expletives about the midfielder, Keane received a five-match ban and a considerably larger 150,000 fine for his troubles.

The United captain retired from the game in 2006 after a short six-month stint at Celtic where he plied his trade following the termination of his contract sanctioned by Manchester United whilst the Irishman was injured in November 2005. The reasoning behind such a shocking transfer story was due to comments Keane made about teammates on MUTV, the club's television channel after a humiliating 4-1 defeat at the hands of Middlesbrough in the league at the Riverside in October 2005.

Keane has never strayed too far from the headlines. That MUTV outburst criticised a number of players including the likes of Rio Ferdinand, John O'Shea, Alan Smith and Darren Fletcher. He has, in the past, received fines by the club for incidents such as elbowing Jason McAteer in a Premier League clash against Sunderland in the 2002-03 season which was sparked by Keane's fight with Irish national team boss Mick McCarthy.

The Irish captain left the World Cup camp prior to the tournament in 2002 after complaining about the team's preparations and the diet that preceded the group stages. Ireland would go onto the second round without Keane in another incident documented by his 2002 autobiography.

He even criticised the fans of Manchester United after a Champions League group stage match in 2000 with Dynamo Kiev, labelling them quiet during spells of the match. His aggression is epitomised by the record which he jointly holds—the amount of red cards received in English football which stands at thirteen.

However, Keane has been lauded by many critics despite his anger problems. He was inducted into the English football Hall of Fame in 2004 before being added to the FIFA 100 list by Pele in the twilight stages of his career at Old Trafford. The list of personal honours coupled with the honours for Manchester United, Nottingham Forest and Celtic must serve as a testament to the great midfielder that he truly was.

Referring back to one of Keane's less prouder moments in football—the Alf-Inge Haaland challenge and the publication of his autobiography a year later, what if Roy Keane had been given a lifetime playing ban for ending Alf-Inge Haaland's career upon the publication of his book in August 2002?

The news is met with widespread hysteria at Old Trafford as Sir Alex Ferguson is left with just a few days to replace Keane in time for the upcoming 2002-

03 season. On the eve of their Premier League tie with West Brom, Luis Figo was snapped up from Real Madrid for a fee of 34 million as Sir Alex Ferguson looked to throw more money into a season which already contained the 30 million transfer of Rio Ferdinand from Leeds.

Figo would make his debut away at the Stadium of Light, assisting Ryan Giggs with a couple of goals as United claimed a 3-2 win in the north-east. That would become better known as one of the highlights of the Portuguese playmaker's career as he would be sold to Inter Milan for a bargain at 11.5 million in 2007. United's only honours in that period came through a slim League Cup final win over Wigan in 2006 and a Premier League campaign wrapped up on goal difference in 2005, as they beat Chelsea by just seven goals in the tightest Premier League season ever.

The big money splurged on Figo was almost costing a knight of the British realm in Alex Ferguson a job at the club. After Figo's sale to Inter Milan, Roy Keane had soon announced that he had captured Zlatan Ibrahimovic for his club, Bayern Munich for the start of the upcoming 2007-08 season.

Keane had been in football management on the continent since 2004, when he announced himself as a full-time manager with the signing of Cristiano Ronaldo for Bayern as his first player, snatching him from the jaws of Sir Alex and Manchester United for a 15 million price tag. Whilst one Portuguese midfielder was flopping at Old Trafford in Luis Figo, the next generation in Cristiano Ronaldo was making waves in the Bundesliga, assisting two goals on his debut against Stuttgart in August 2004.

Keane secured Champions League football in his

opening season as Bayern Munich manager as early as February 2005 before wrapping up the title in early April with a 4-1 demolition of Hertha Berlin. Keane's policy was simple; buy the Bundesliga's best talent before polishing off his side with names from elsewhere in Europe. The duo of Miroslav Klose and Dimitar Berbatov were both signed from Werder Bremen and Bayer Leverkusen respectively whilst Lukas Podolski joined them later on in the season.

Frank Lampard was a purchase that couldn't be passed up, according to Roy Keane in a 2009 interview with *Sky Sports*, four years after his signature was claimed by the former United player. The ex-Chelsea midfielder provided the key that unlocked European success for the renovated German outfit.

An undefeated group stage claimed the prospect of Juventus in the knockout stages as Bayern eliminated them on the final day, allowing Club Brugge into the second round. The final group stage contest was retrospectively identified as a highlight according to the manager at a post-season dinner in Munich.

Miroslav Klose, who had scored a hat-trick for Germany the week prior to the away contest in Turin, was benched which left the German furious at Keane but the manager's little secret in Lukas Podolski shone through, scoring twice and assisting Klose as he came off the bench with Ronaldo netting the other in an outstanding 4-1 away win in Italy.

That set the precedent for the remainder of the season for Bayern who claimed the Bundesliga a week later than the previous season but managed to rack up seven more points than the previous term. In the Champions League, Keane took the scalps of A.C. Milan and Lyon before a Frank Lampard penalty was enough to see off Barcelona in the semi-final, with a slender 1-0 aggregate victory enough to seal Keane's first managerial UEFA Champions League final.

Keane would see off old foes, Arsenal, in such a routine display which seemed harrowing for English football compared to their German counterparts as Bayern romped to a 4-0 drubbing of the English side in Paris. Bayern might have been the only German side remaining when the knockout stage began but they flew the flag for Germany and subsequently dominated the tournament from start to finish as Klose claimed the top scorer prize with 13 goals in 14 games.

The only piece of silverware which scuppered Keano and his Bayern side was the German Cup as they were dispatched by Borussia Dortmund at the semi-final stage. They would get their revenge with a 3-0 whitewash in the Super Cup at the beginning of the following season.

Meanwhile, Ferguson recorded his lowest finish in the Premier League of fourth which only marginally confirmed Champions League football for the 2006-07 season. That's where Roy Keane would be re-introduced to the Old Trafford atmosphere and his former manager in Sir Alex.

The 2006-07 season would be better known as Cristiano Ronaldo's breakthrough season amongst the Bayern fans. His hat-trick against Dortmund in the Super Cup final was only a slender portion of what the Bayern fans could expect over the coming seasons. He would net forty-one goals in the season as Bayern claimed the domestic double as Keane lapped up all the praise for bleeding youth into what was slowly becoming a star-studded line-up in Munich.

The Champions League would be left unable to retain

thanks to a slice of mind games from Keane's former employer—Manchester United in 2007 though.

After another undefeated group stage campaign at the beginning of the season, Bayern were now favourites to claim another Champions League crown and added to their fire power by signing David Villa in January. Villa scored four times over the course of the quarter final tie against Real Madrid which, after a 7-2 aggregate humiliation for the Spanish, had the Manchester United fans quaking as they learned of their semi-final opponents.

An all-English final looked unlikely as Liverpool were thrown Barcelona in the other semi-final but this trophy seemed Bayern's to lose. The Allianz Arena was the home of the first leg where a tremendous free-kick from Cristiano Ronaldo settled the match. Bayern would take a 1-0 lead to Manchester, much to the delight of Roy Keane as he celebrated with his star names on the pitch after the final whistle.

Ferguson lapped up Keane's ability to coach a side from his technical area, praising the likes of Villa, Ronaldo and Lampard—labelling them the new Holy Trinity, after the original trinity of Law, Best & Charlton. Keane hit back in a following pre-match press conference, stating that they had already overshadowed the accomplishments made by those famous group of United players in the sixties. Keane claimed the evidence in this sensationalist statement was all thanks to Bayern's dominance over Europe and Germany over the past couple of years.

Whilst the Manchester United manager kept largely quiet in the match's build-up to his response to his former player, it was clear that he had touched a nerve; he was under Keane's skin. The Bayern manager replied by implementing all three of his apparent 'holy trinity' rendition up front with Klose and Podolski also in the extremely attacking line-up.

All pundits in the ground were perplexed with Keane's tactics both before and after the match as Bayern went onto lose 4-1, losing their first European match for three years. The 2006-07 Champions League crown would ultimately go to Barcelona but Ferguson had the last laugh over his former player in Keane.

Bayern would be back with Keane at the helm and back with a bang in the following season's Champions League, conceding just three goals in the entirety of the competition as they humiliated Barcelona 4-1 in the 2008 Champions League final. Keane would set more precedents for himself, achieving successive treble-winning seasons as Bayern became the first side to retain the Champions League since A.C. Milan at the start of the nineties when David Villa scored a goal in extra time to beat Chelsea 3-2 in 2009 Champions League final in Rome.

Keane would lift all four of the next Bundesliga titles but would resign as Bayern manager with immediate effect in 2013 as he claimed his fourth Champions League crown, his first in four years, beating Bob Paisley's record of three titles in the process. Keane was reportedly bought out of his position by A.S. Monaco who seemingly had money to throw at anything that could kick a football, or that was associated with the sport.

Although the official quote from the Bayern Munich website claimed that Roy Keane left on mutual terms, the reports in his opening few months as Monaco manager claimed he had left due to a 15 million buyout from the French side.

Keane stated, in his first press conference as Monaco manager that he wanted to bring football to Monte Carlo, wanted to bring the world to the south of France. In terms of his signings, he did so at an alarming rate.

Falcao from Atletico Madrid was purchased for a near fifty million euros whilst the likes of Wayne Rooney, Nemanja Vidic, Iker Casillas, Jordi Alba, Cesc Fabregas and David Beckham were all added to the ranks at the French club by the end of the summer as the Roy Keane managerial reign in the small French principality was beginning at a rapid pace.

In their first season back in Ligue 1, Monaco would win the title immediately with the front three of Rooney, Falcao and Fabregas generating 87 goals between them as they lost just once in the entire season and went onto accumulate 103 points. While Roy Keane was taking Monaco to their first Champions League campaign in almost a decade, Ferguson was retiring, handing the reins over to David Moyes for the beginning of the 2014-15 season.

Keane would be immortalised in Monte Carlo, bringing them successive Ligue 1 trophies and three Champions League titles across the 2010's as the new era of football certainly looked balanced in the rich hands of Monaco. Roy Keane had only just begun, it seemed.

13

Zizou

A couple of chapters back, I mentioned how Roberto Baggio could be in the greatest eleven in Italian football. In terms of Zinedine Zidane he is almost certain of a berth in France's greatest ever eleven alongside 1984 European Championship winner Michel Platini in the middle of the pitch. Zidane helped France take home their first ever FIFA World Cup in 1998 with two goals in a final demolition of Brazil in Paris.

Zidane was in possibly the best French side to ever compete at a major tournament, along with Marcel Desailly, Fabien Barthez, Laurent Blanc, Emmanuel Petit, Thierry Henry, David Trezeguet and Didier Deschamps, the list goes on. They became the first side since the West German outfit of the 1970's to complete a European Championship and World Cup double when they clawed the European Championship away from Italy in 2000 at the turn of the 21st century.

Zidane was a major catalyst, particularly at the host's World Cup winning tournament in 1998. He was lapping up all the plaudits for his club side Juventus, appearing in successive losing UEFA Champions League finals against Real Madrid, who would be his next club, and Borussia Dortmund in the late nineties.

A couple of Serie A divisional titles, personal accolades and those two international trophies with France later and he was being shipped to Spain for a world record transfer fee. A reported 75 million euros was the fee paid by Real Madrid to pry Zidane away from Juventus, resulting in a huge profit for the Italian club.

Zidane finally won the only trophy that had eluded him so far in his career which was the UEFA Champions League. Zidane scored the winning goal in Glasgow in a 2-1 win over Bayer Leverkusen—a goal still remarked about today as being one of the greatest goals in the Champions League, if not the whole of European football.

The stage that the Frenchman pulled off the awkward volley—with his weaker foot, was so important that it magnified the ability and class of the goal. The Galacticos were formed in Madrid as the likes of Raul, Ronaldo, Figo, Guti, Beckham, McManaman, Casillas, Roberto Carlos and the like all turned out for Real by the 2003-04 season, a season prior to Zidane collecting his first and only La Liga crown in 2003.

With the star-power that Real possessed during that period of time, there's a wonder that Zidane didn't collect anymore silverware for his side. He picked up the FIFA World Player of the Year award three times in 1998, 2000 and 2003 and the Ballon d'Or in 1998, emulating Michel Platini's love-affair with the trophy in the mid-eighties. Fans voted for him as the greatest European player of the past fifty years in UEFA's Golden Jubilee Poll in 2004.

All of the personal accolades had been achieved by Zidane but there will always be one moment for the Frenchman that will taint his entire career. Zidane announced his complete retirement from the game for after the 2006 FIFA World Cup and he had captained his side to the final, even lifting the Golden Ball award for the best player in the tournament.

However, his last act on a football pitch was to deliver a headbutt to Italian defender Marco Materazzi resulting in his red card and, later on in the game, an Italian victory on penalties as Zidane trudged past the World Cup in Berlin, the trophy that he wouldn't be able to lift again.

Now, Zinedine Zidane is qualifying on a coaching course and will take up the mantle of coaching Real Madrid's youth academy. Without his name in the elite band of players to have won the trophy twice, what could have been? **What if Zinedine Zidane didn't headbutt Marco Materazzi to get red carded in the 2006 FIFA World Cup final in Berlin?**

The ball broke out for a flaccid Italian counter attack which soon broke down and after a dull second period of extra time, the FIFA World Cup final went to penalties for only the second time in its history between France and Italy inside the Olympic Stadium in Berlin. The host of commentators in the executive seats in the stadium were discussing how nobody wanted to become a villain like Baggio did in the 1994 final courtesy of his missed spot kick against Brazil in the only other shootout in a World Cup final.

Zidane stepped up first and coolly slotted his penalty into the bottom corner, a transition from the cheeky attempt in normal time which opened the scoring. Both teams exchanged penalties without fault until Fabio Grosso, Italy's hero from the semi-final win over the hosts, Germany, stepped up.

The full-back blazed the ball high and wide which confirmed France's second World Cup title, their first in eight years as Zidane lifted the trophy high in Berlin.

After the celebrations had died down in the French

camp, World Cup winning manager, Raymond Domenech resigned as a successful coach which left many of the French media awaiting the freshly retired Zinedine Zidane to become his natural successor. At the age of 34, Zidane had no coaching experience whatsoever but that didn't deter the French football association from announcing him as the new head coach in the late July of 2006 following the successful tournament.

Many of the world's media were hedging their bets on Zidane's reign not to last the full upcoming European Championships qualifying campaign for the tournament which would culminate in Austria and Switzerland which were two years away. After a 2-1 loss to Scotland at the Stade de France, many questioned his ability to manage a group of individuals.

Coming off the back of such a euphoric day which was the World Cup final win in July, many were calling for Zidane's sacking as he left them in fourth place behind Italy, Scotland and Ukraine by November, just four months after France's second World Cup was confirmed. An away win in Italy seemed to soothe some nerves around France as they leapt to second place in the table but would plummet like a stone after successive defeats to Ukraine and Lithuania in early 2007 as they failed to qualify for a tournament for the first time since the 1994 FIFA World Cup.

They wouldn't part with their dear beloved superstar, purely based on his image in France as the national football association saw fit to stick with the Algerian-born playmaker turned manager for the FIFA World Cup qualifying campaign.

Being pitted against the European Champions in Germany for their opening qualifier did Zidane no favours whatsoever. The Olympic Stadium that Zidane lifted the World Cup trophy at just two summers previously became the setting for another famous French win as Nicolas Anelka bagged two goals in a 3-0 away victory.

That would be one of the only high points of France's entire qualification campaign; successive draws to Bosnia, Slovenia and Israel left France in a lowly third place going into 2009. Germany's revenge victory in Paris in March 2009 didn't help the cause either as France realistically needed to win their remaining matches to qualify outright for the tournament in South Africa.

The away trips in June to far flung places such as Bosnia and Israel were successful as France marginally achieved a play-off place, holding off Slovenia for second place, as the French notched up seven points from their final three qualifiers. Zidane heralded a new generation of French players as they steamrolled through Slovakia, winning 4-0 in Bratislava following a 2-1 home defeat.

Whichever way you looked at it, Zidane's French side were extremely lucky to make the 2010 FIFA World Cup but they were handsomely rewarded with a seemingly straight-forward group containing the hosts, South Africa along with Mexico and Uruguay.

A loss to Uruguay thanks to a Diego Forlan brace, coupled with a 0-0 stalemate with Mexico had France needing a large win over the hosts who were in search of their own win to qualify. A three-goal win would help them overtake Mexico in second place and face Argentina in the knockout stages. Thierry Henry and

Samir Nasri scored goals as France sauntered into a 3-1 half-time lead, needing just one more goal to seal their passage into the second round.

Hearing the news that Mexico were losing 4-0 to Uruguay boosted the French confidence further and sure enough, France were served another major slice of luck.

On the 88th minute mark, a free-kick was drifted into an offside Gael Clichy who tucked the ball into the net as he wheeled away in celebration. Despite the South African protests, the French won the match 4-1 and would be pitted against Diego Maradona's Argentina.

Zidane had experienced a final game qualification to the knockout stages in the previous World Cup as he had to sit on the sidelines and hoped France beat Togo to qualify. Now he was aiming for a second successive World Cup, France's third in twelve years. Many of the French media backed Zidane to the hilt, but the world's media wrote off all French hopes, they were placed tenth favourites with SkyBet out of the sixteen remaining teams in the second round.

If Zidane had any hair remaining on his head, he would be pulling out a few days later in the second round clash with Argentina. It was truly nail-biting stuff, accompanied with various shots of French fans actually biting their nails during extra time as France somehow hung on, despite being bombarded and camped in their own half all game, they would have to claim their quarter final berth via a penalty shootout.

In the previous shootout they contested, France won the World Cup, this time they celebrated like they had won the World Cup when Gabriel Heinze fluffed his lines and France progressed to the quarter finals, winning 5-3 in the shootout. Zidane's French side were becoming resurgent, albeit with a helping hand from a higher power as the tournament favourites in, France's next opponents, Germany crumbled thanks to an early Per Mertesacker own goal in their quarter-final.

Zidane was quick to highlight that France's success came from the highly regimented defensive line, which had shut out Germany and Argentina despite them launching the kitchen sink at them during the latter stages of the tournament.

The semi-final offered France to the new tournament favourites in Spain. France's fortunes had transformed and by half-time their supporters inside the stadium in Durban didn't feel too lucky. A quick-fire double from David Villa inside four opening first-half minutes left France red-faced after their poor displays throughout the tournament had finally been revealed to the world.

The slouching French side trudged out into the half-time break, into their dressing room but returned visibly revitalised. Fifty-minutes later and the world's media was left utterly baffled and devoid of any coherent thoughts, France had escaped again. How?

Franck Ribery was hoisted onto Zidane's shoulders during the on-pitch celebration as the winger's hat-trick effectively sunk Spain's aspirations of a first World Cup final in their footballing history. Conversely, this allowed France the ability to realistically dream for the first time that they would retain the World Cup in South Africa.

Despite the arduous journey Zinedine Zidane had made from his last World Cup final to this one, Holland were still deemed the favourites to take home their first ever World Cup trophy in Johannesburg.

A couple of tackles were flying in, none too uncharacteristic with the Dutch side who had played the dirty style of football under van Basten that wasn't evident during the Johan Cruyff days of 'Total Football' in the 1970's. However, when Nigel de Jong unleashed a kick that the Karate Kid would've been proud of into the heart of Florent Malouda, the referee, Howard Webb only saw fit to book the Manchester City player. Tempers soon boiled over in the Soccer City stadium.

After a brief discussion, if you call label it as calmly as that, Zidane pushed the Dutch manager, van Basten away from him. Both coaches got a warning as the fourth official told Zidane to cool down in his seat to disembroil the pair of managers from their heated debate on the sideline. As the French manager was walking away, van Basten could be seen in the background talking to him, that's when the anger spilled out over the touchline.

Zidane launched himself at Marco van Basten as the Euro 1988 winner cut a crumpled figure on the South African turf on the halfway line as Zidane pushed the Dutch coach once more before throwing his head into his chest. Van Basten slumped to the ground, clutching his heart as the French dugout and supporters inside the stadium collectively winced, Zidane was sent off and forced to watch the remainder of the match from high up in the stadium.

Holland went onto win the match 2-0, as Marco van Basten paraded around Johannesburg with the Dutch's first ever World Cup.

Zidane would never grace a football pitch again; he was labelled as 'Le Mechant Totale' which translates to the Total Villain in French. He would be sacked with immediate effect from the football association and never coached or played ever again; it was a sad career ending for Zidane who passed up on the opportunity to win his third FIFA World Cup with an illustrious French side.

Meanwhile, for the national side, they crashed out at the group stages of successive tournaments in the European Championships in 2012 and the World Cup in Brazil two years later. The French still hadn't fully recovered from what Zidane had donated to them—a resilient but disgraced footballing outfit. He would be appointed as a Director of Football at Real Madrid for his services to the club some years previously.

14

They Think It's All Over ... It Is Now

We, the British, can thank Kenneth Wolstenholme for that famous quote which preceded the greatest goal, in terms of importance, of English footballing history as Geoff Hurst wrapped up England's one and only World Cup at Wembley in 1966. Hurst, who was deputising for the injured Tottenham Hotspur striker, Jimmy Greaves, rattled in the third of his hat-trick as delirious supporters took to the field to celebrate.

Hurst was subsequently knighted and still remains the only player to score a hat-trick in a FIFA World Cup final. The Germans still argue to this day about Geoff Hurst's 101st minute goal which put England into a 3-2 extra time lead, whether it crossed the line or not. This debate was re-opened when Frank Lampard was cruelly robbed of the chance to equalise in the 2010 FIFA World Cup second round encounter with the Germans in Bloemfontein.

Lampard's goal, thanks to the numerous replays, was adjudged to have cross the line by everybody watching in their homes, pubs or bars, everybody in the stadium, including the commentators and the smattering of the world's media housed in the stadium. The only people who didn't see it cross the line, were the most important people on the pitch — the officials.

In the 1966 final, there wasn't the luxury of continuous replays on offer to show the viewing public whether or not Geoff Hurst had fired England into a lead or not. The Swiss referee, Gottfried Dienst had to consult his Soviet linesman, who in the heat of the moment confirmed the ball crossed the line.

Down the years, we have never been too certain that the ball did cross the line until technology recently has been able to tell us that it didn't, and the linesman, who didn't share a common language between the referee, was rushed into a decision and was conclusively wrong.

England would effectively steal the FIFA World Cup away from Germany at Wembley Stadium in front of almost 100,000 people and secure their only World Cup triumph to date as the Germans claimed daylight robbery.

The 'wingless wonders' of England, led by Bobby Moore lifted the famous trophy in front of the Queen and the adoring English public inside the capital's centrepiece stadium.

England would go onto to record a near miss in the 1990 World Cup final, losing out to their old enemy, the Germans, in a penalty shootout. Whilst Germany would record another two FIFA World Cups to their tally, England haven't made a tournament final since the 1966 final, but it could have all been so different.

What if Gottfried Dienst ruled out Geoff Hurst's goal in the FIFA World Cup final in 1966?

The English appeals are futile as the Swiss referee carried on with the action in extra time at Wembley stadium. Wolstenholme in the BBC commentary box would remain furious for the rest of the extra time period, as would England manager Alf Ramsey who constantly berated the officials, including and especially the Soviet linesman after the match who couldn't reach a decision which allowed the successful German counter-attack.

From the counter, German forward and captain Uwe Seeler nets what would be the winning goal as West Germany claim their second FIFA World Cup title, winning 3-2 as Bobby Moore and co. would only leaving with the loser's medals as Germany celebrated on the Wembley turf.

Four years later, and after a semi-final exit in the European Championships in 1968, England became more determined than ever to claim the prize which they still claimed at the 1970 tournament that was rightfully theirs. A Geoff Hurst goal would sink the Romanians in a slender 1-0 win in their opening match of the World Cup staged in Mexico.

Forthcoming for England would be the famous Brazil, looking to add to their record of two World Cup titles. Pele was their danger man but, fortunately for England, he seemed off his game in Guadalajara and was marked off the pitch by centre-half, Bobby Moore, almost literally at some points in the contest by the robust defender.

A tremendous Gordon Banks save from a Pele header preserved the stalemate but it would be transformed into a win by a late Bobby Charlton winner from distance which had England fans dreaming about the World Cup they believe they should've lifted four years previously.

They qualified from the group with ease after a 4-0 demolition job over Czechoslovakia to reach the quarter final thanks to a double from Jimmy Greaves who returned to the national side after a two year absence after the European Championships.

Peru were the quarter-final opponents and after the

victory over Brazil, England were swiftly becoming the tournament favourites, even over holders West Germany. A routine 3-0 win over Peru thanks to goals from Alan Mullery and Geoff Hurst booked England's place in the semi-final with the enemy. West Germany.

A tactical game was deadlocked even by the time ninety minutes had ticked over with the two powerhouses of Bobby Moore and Franz Beckenbauer, of Alf Ramsey and Helmut Schon jostling for power in the semi-final tie. One of those powerhouses would open the game's goalscoring as Beckenbauer unleashed one of the goals of the tournament just four minutes into extra time.

Ramsey was forced to make an impromptu team-talk on the Mexican turf at half-time in extra time. Details about the team talk have been debated down the decades but whatever Ramsey said, it worked. Martin Peters netted an equaliser shortly after the break before Bobby Charlton got a winning goal only two minutes from time. England were destined for successive World Cup finals through the management of Ramsey.

Whilst Ramsey was reportedly in line for a knighthood upon the conclusion of the tournament, there was still work to do on the pitch. Brazil were the opponents once again. Geoff Hurst was benched after niggling doubts about the striker's fitness which allowed Jimmy Greaves one last fling at international football.

Jairzinho and Pele were frightening the English supporters inside Mexico City with their dazzling ability but the inevitable struck on 27 minutes as Pele simply waltzed through the English defence, even through the legend of Bobby Moore.

England were faced with another mountainous task

to overcome another established national side. Ramsey would win English hearts over again as he paraded up and down the sideline, out of his technical area and dugout, bursting instructions out to his eleven lions.

The tabloids would forever dub the 1970 World Cup side as the Eleven Lions as two goals from Jimmy Greaves followed by a Geoff Hurst goal capped off four years of hurt in the England camp, they had finally brought home the FIFA World Cup, beating the mighty Brazil 3-1, who had never been beaten in a World Cup final prior to the fateful day in Mexico City. England were back.

Ramsey decided at the eleventh hour to stay in his position as the England manager. He claimed in a 1983 interview with the BBC that the moment he decided arrived when "we stepped off the plane coming back from Mexico, everybody was so jubilant; I couldn't leave all that behind."

The 1974 World Cup group stage was a walk in the park for the English as they disposed of an East German side before humiliating Australia 7-0 in West Berlin. Chile escaped punishment as they held Ramsey's Eleven Lions to a 0-0 draw in Hamburg. England topped their subsequent group, leaving preparing for a final against Johan Cryuff's Holland. 32-year old veteran, Geoff Hurst was rivalling the playmaker for the player of the tournament accolade after his five goals throughout the finals.

However, a Cryuff masterclass upset the odds as England fell to a 2-0 defeat in their third successive FIFA World Cup final. Ramsey resigned after the tournament and England didn't qualify for the 1976 European Championships, but were represented in the following World Cup campaign in Argentina by Don

Revie who was elected to lead England into a new era by the Football Association.

England battled through a tough group containing the hosts along with Italy and Hungary. The Magyars were the only club that England beat in the first group stage, as Revie's side were held by both the Italians and Argentine to draws, booking their place in the next stage by a marginal goal average. Kevin Keegan was the architect of a large portion of England's success.

Two goals from the Hamburg attacking midfielder against Brazil effectively knocked them out before eliminating both Peru and Austria from the final group stage as they shaped up to meet Holland in yet another FIFA World Cup final. Not since 1962 had there been a World Cup final without England in the match.

Sixteen years later from that Brazil triumph in Chile, England were again meticulously picked apart by Johan Cryuff who showed all the class that he possessed four years previously, and then some. A double for the Dutch master coupled with more goals left England on the wrong end of their worst ever World Cup defeat, losing 5-1 to the Dutch in Argentina. England wouldn't recover for a long time.

After early exits in the European Championships in 1980 and the subsequent World Cup in 1982, Don Revie was sacked, leaving Bobby Robson to pick up the pieces of a broken England camp. They would be heartbroken in the 1984 European Championships semi-final, losing out to France before failure to qualify for the 1986 FIFA World Cup left a lot of doubters in the British media about Robson's talent to coach such a prestigious national side.

Further journalists were calling for Robson to stand down as England manager when in 1988, at the

European Championships, they were dumped out of the group stages by the Soviet Union. The Dutch ran riot once more, winning their fourth major tournament of the past two decades.

Bobby Robson and his men qualified by the skin of their teeth for the World Cup in 1990 which was being hosted in Italy. An away win over Switzerland allowed them to qualify automatically for the tournament when it looked like England would have to watch Ireland in the World Cup as their summer's entertainment.

Paul Gascoigne would rectify this with the winning goal against Ireland in the opening group stage match. A win over Egypt effectively booked England's passage into the knockout stages but before they could think about a date with Belgium, Holland were next.

Bobby Robson made no mistake of letting his England players know in pre-match press conferences that the Dutch were dangerous opponents. After citing the 1970's World Cup defeats on the eve of their encounter, he told the press that his side would wash away the heartache from those final defeats and give them another final with England to talk about.

England would lose 3-1 to Holland.

Robson, remained a little red-faced about his previous statement in the now infamous press conference. Although, in the next meeting with the press, he saw fit not to discuss second round opponents Belgium. England romped home to a Gary Lineker inspired 4-0 victory over the Belgians with a 3-0 mauling of Cameroon followed in the quarter finals. England were looking forward to the prospects of a possible final in Rome.

Until, that is, they were lumbered with West

Germany. The Germans were looking efficient and many backed them to triumph in the tournament. They were the favourites but only slightly ahead of England, after their brutal knockout stage performances which, to some extent, shot fear into the hearts of the Germans.

Sure enough, two David Platt goals coupled with two German equalisers left a tantalising game in the balance as it was seemingly heading towards extra time. Would the famous 1966 final be emulated? A lunging Paul Gascoigne tackle had the referee flirting with the yellow card in his back pocket which would've suspended the midfielder for the final. However, the referee decided to warn 'Gazza' about his future tackles.

Gascoigne would fire England towards a fifth FIFA World Cup final, still a record held to this day, as he netted five minutes from the end of the second half. There was no need for extra time as Bobby Robson danced in Turin, writing adequate back pages for the British tabloids the following day. England were embarking on their first major tournament final in twelve years, this time Holland weren't standing in their way.

Instead, the hosts, Italy took up the position as the opponents that Robson would have to beat to become immortalised in English footballing history. There were already plans in place for a bronze statue to be erected the following year in Robson's honour, which would be all but confirmed if he could win England's second FIFA World Cup.

The crowd were easily in favour of the hosts, with an almost 80/20 split inside the Stadio Olimpico in Rome. Salvatore Schillaci burned England with an early goal but the scar would be healed almost immediately with a strike from John Barnes a mere eight minutes later. England were in the driving seat and through all of their attacking play and efforts on goal, they were dumbfounded to not be in the lead by the full-time whistle was sounded.

Memories of 1966 came flooding back, the extra time and possible penalties were looming, was there a contentious decision in the following thirty minutes or would Italy kill off any English dreams of another World Cup?

David Platt had the answer for Bobby, soon to be Sir Bobby. The forward swivelled in the area, wrong-footing a group of Italian defenders and before 73,000 fans in Rome, curled an effort into the far corner of the bulging net. Platt had won the World Cup for England and for Bobby Robson with his 115th minute goal which had England partying in the ashen faces of the Italians, they had beat them in their own backyard, just like Germans did in 1966.

Robson would coach England to glory in the 1992 European Championships as they defeated Germany in the final before stumbling to an embarrassing 1994 FIFA World Cup quarter-final defeat to Sweden. Robson would hand the power over to Terry Venables, who after successive semi-final defeats in the late nineties at the hands of the Czech Republic and Brazil led England to a second European Championship crown in 2000 before retiring.

Meanwhile, Germany would have to wait until the 2006 FIFA World Cup to win their first piece of silverware since 1966, beating Italy in their own Olympic Stadium in Berlin as England looked on, as defeated quarter finalists.

15

Marching on Together

At the turn of the recent millennium, Leeds United were reaching a height through manager David O'Leary that hadn't been achieved by the West Yorkshire club since the height of their powers in the 1970's, in which they fell in a European Cup final to Gerd Muller's Bayern Munich.

A league title was won in the last Old First Division season prior to the birth of the Premier League but Leeds wouldn't enjoy a period of dominance like the 1970's under Don Revie who would later go onto manage the England national side.

However, in the latter stages of the 1990's, a youthful group of players, almost akin to the 1992 FA Youth Cup winning side of Manchester United, in terms of the quality, came through the Leeds ranks. The likes of Alan Smith, Harry Kewell, Ian Harte, Paul Robinson and Jonathan Woodgate all shone through the academy whilst Rio Ferdinand, Nigel Martyn, Michael Bridges, Lucas Radebe, Danny Mills and David Batty also added necessary experience at Elland Road at the turn of the century.

All of the aforementioned, barring Michael Bridges, would go onto represent their countries on many occasions, whilst others have collected accolades such as Premier League titles through Alan Smith and Rio Ferdinand at Manchester United and the Champions League titles in the case of Rio Ferdinand and Harry Kewell at Manchester United and Liverpool respectively in the forthcoming years.

There was a period around the new millennium in which Leeds almost broke the dominance shared by Manchester United and Arsenal, threatening that by maintaining a top five position through 1999 to 2002.

Despite a European semi-final against Galatasaray in the UEFA Cup which of course ended in tragedy when two Leeds supporters were killed by opposition fans in Istanbul, the West Yorkshire club maintained their threat in the domestic competitions. They also reached the final four against Valencia in May 2001 in their first UEFA Champions League campaign in eight years, almost equalling their record in Europe's top club competition.

Peter Risdale, the Leeds United chairman, announced debt, following the impressive run in the Champions League. The debts had gathered through loans which couldn't be repaid after they marginally missed out on UEFA Champions League qualification for two successive years in 2001 and 2002.

Consequently, Leeds had to sell the best crop of players they had in some time, with the money generated from Rio Ferdinand's thirty million switch to Manchester United along with the departure of Bowyer to West Ham, Woodgate to Newcastle and Harry Kewell to Liverpool all raising funds to keep the club afloat. O'Leary's successors in Terry Venables and Peter Reid couldn't quell the downslide despite the signings of Robbie Fowler, Robbie Keane, Nick Barmby and Jody Morris. The West Yorkshire club plummeted down into the Championship in 2004, placing 19th in the Premier League, only being propped up by Wolverhampton Wanderers just three years after a Champions League semi-final at Elland

Road against Valencia.

The turning point for the club following relegation came in May 2006 when they lost out to Aidy Boothroyd's Watford in the Championship play-off final at the Millennium Stadium and would never recover fully. The financial position would worsen as Leeds were demoted further down the English leagues into the third tier the following season for the first time in their history and would be docked fifteen points upon relegation.

After two play-off heartbreaks, Leeds were finally promoted back into the second tier in 2010 and now ply their trade in the Championship. It still remains a gulf of where they were just a mere decade or so previously.

What if Risdale, in 2001, didn't take out any loans and Leeds didn't have to relinquish any of their star players?

David O'Leary applauded his players off the Mestalla pitch as they headed out of their first Champions League campaign under his reign at the semi-final stage in May 2001. The former Ireland international proclaimed in the press conference that he was "proud of the young lads," also wish that they could "hopefully get our head down for the final two matches in the league to make sure we can do this again next year."

O'Leary and his players would be celebrating come May 19th, 2001 — the final day of the Premier League season of 2000-01. A commanding 4-0 win at home to Bradford City thanks to a sublime couple of goals from Mark Viduka was coupled by a 3-1 win over Leicester City on the final day. Thanks to Liverpool's failure to win away at Southampton, Leeds booked their plane tickets for a qualifying round tie against Finnish team, Haka in August after they placed third in the league — the final berth for next season's Champions League.

Despite much speculation surrounding a lot of Premier League players heading to Elland Road in the summer, David O'Leary looked towards the continent to find the experience that his campaign in Europe craved.

Sure enough, a 21 million pound fee was being paid to Lazio as Leeds pipped Juventus to his signature in the summer of 2001. Nedved made an instant impact, assisting a couple of goals before scoring in a 6-1 demolition of Haka in the Champions League qualifiers. O'Leary would lead his men into the group stages after a 11-2 aggregate win, whilst slightly under-performing domestically.

After Leeds had surrendered sixth position in November thanks to a humiliating 2-1 home defeat at the hands of Ipswich, they had recorded a fifth win in six European contests, beating Borussia Dortmund in Germany to qualify for the second group stage.

Leeds couldn't face Valencia due to their non-participation in the tournament but instead were fed their compatriots and eight-time champions in Real Madrid. An opener in the Bernabeu terrified the Leeds fans who, being interviewed by *Sky Sports*, stated they'd be ecstatic if they lost by the odd goal in Madrid.

Harry Kewell would score the solitary goal in Spain as Leeds won 1-0 in the Bernabeu and subsequently waltzed into the knockout stages, recording 12 points from an unbeaten six outings which included a 2-0 with over Juventus as Pavel Nedved scored a goal in front of the fans which could have been singing his name on that very night.

They finished top of their respective group, shading their position by a couple of goals from Real Madrid as Juventus and Borussia Dortmund both failed to qualify in what was labelled the group of death for the second group stage round.

O'Leary earmarked his own club as the favourites even in his post-match press conference against Bayern Munich where they fell 2-1 in Germany. Nonetheless, the press agreed, Leeds were still the favourites to qualify and they were making a late surge up the table too.

When the knockout stages swung around in April, Leeds had climbed from eighth to third and were hunting down Arsenal's position in the Premier League. Despite being upset by second tier club, Coventry City in the League Cup, O'Leary was aiming for Champions League qualification through the league as well as either the FA Cup or the highest European accolade for a manager—the Champions League which was, according to the Irishman, on the Leeds United horizon.

Many journalists at the time agreed that the Irishman was being "too ambitious" and was "going to disappoint a lot of the Leeds boardroom come the end of the season".

However, a four day period at Old Trafford soon turned the heads of a lot of the press. Manchester United, who had seemingly wrapped up another league title, were thirteen points clear when Leeds visited in mid-April. After a courageous and determined display, Leeds were still trailing the champions by a goal. However, in the second half the Yorkshire club put one over the Manchester outfit as

Alan Smith's hat-trick married with a Michael Bridges finish steamrolled the high-flying club who were unlikely to be shot down from the perch in that particularly.

Nevertheless, Leeds had created a highlight with their 4-1 win away at Old Trafford, which placed them second with four matches remaining and halted what would have been a title party that night in Manchester and sent ripples of their quality to the viewing public throughout Europe.

O'Leary was about to create another highlight in the Leeds United supporter's memory bank in the FA Cup semi-final at Old Trafford just mere days later. Aston Villa were their opponents with Liverpool a potential challenge in the final in Cardiff. Harry Kewell sent Villa packing with an early brace which helped Leeds to a 3-1 win in the north-west as Leeds confirmed their place in an FA Cup final for the first time since their losing final in 1973 against Sunderland, Leeds' manager still remained adamant that European glory was their top prize but he expressed his want, almost desperation as he noted in post-season, to chalk up some silverware on the board.

Leeds would stumble over the line, finishing second and just a couple of points above Arsenal as Manchester United raced away with the league title. European success was made to wait as they dispatched Bayern Munich on away goals, thanks to a 1-0 win at Elland Road but would eventually succumb to Real Madrid in the semi-finals, losing 3-1 on aggregate in a hard-fought display to another Spanish team in the final four.

O'Leary once more proclaimed his proudness after defeat in Madrid, stating that they will get to a

European final under his tenure.

Leeds would fall at the final hurdle in the FA Cup, losing on penalties after one hundred and twenty minutes of stalemate in Cardiff, Liverpool claiming their seventh FA Cup, and their third domestic cup crown in a matter of fifteen months.

On July 29th, in anticipation of the new 2002-03 season, David O'Leary held a press conference to announce the duo that "would lead Leeds United into European glory" as both Alan Shearer and Fabio Cannavaro appeared, signing for a collective fee of 38 million from Newcastle United and Parma respectively. Mark Viduka and Lucas Radebe were consequently shipped out to French club PSG to fund the deal of the summer whilst Manchester United desperately floundered for a central defender to partner the ageing Laurent Blanc, ultimately penning a deal to sign Marco Materazzi.

That season, Newcastle would claim safety on the last day whilst Leeds United were celebrating another runners-up place, only losing out on the league title on the penultimate day thanks to a 2-0 loss at Highbury which handed Manchester United a fifth successive league title.

Leeds reached a third successive Champions League semi-final, losing out 4-3 on aggregate to A.C. Milan despite Alan Shearer firing Leeds into a 2-0 lead in the early stages of the second leg at the San Siro. Coming back from a 1-1 draw at Elland Road, Milan would net three times in the second half to sink the Yorkshire club's hope of reaching a first Champions League final in twenty-eight years. The English forward led the goalscoring charts with 14 goals for the tournament— a new record, and he helped lift the League Cup in

February 2003 with a 2-1 win over Liverpool in the final, some consolation for losing out on the FA Cup some nine months previously.

O'Leary claimed that, in the summer of 2003, he didn't need to sign anybody to the ranks as the natural development blended in with the new signings would create a winning formula in Europe.

Whilst Leeds sauntered to a place in the knockout stages of that season, they were making much bigger waves in the Premier League that year. Despite being dumped out of the FA Cup at the fifth round stage for the second successive season to West Ham, Alan Shearer retaliated with a four-goal haul away at Stamford Bridge in a 4-2 win which sent them to the top of the league in late February.

After two goalless draws against Aston Villa and Leicester City in late April, the West Yorkshire Premier League title bid was seemingly taking a dive at the worst possible time. Leeds found themselves three points behind Manchester United with three matches remaining, but with an Elland Road showdown with Ferguson and co. on the penultimate day of the season.

O'Leary prepared his troops for an away day at St. James' Park and Alan Shearer scored the decisive winning goal, with muted celebrations in a 1-0 win whilst United could only draw at the Reebok Stadium, being held 2-2 by Bolton.

This left only a point gap when Manchester United travelled to the other side of the Pennines, only needing four points from two games to wrap up a sixth successive league title. An early Ruud van Nistelrooy strike settled Sir Alex Ferguson's nerves in Yorkshire but goals either side of half-time from the talismanic strike partnership of Alan Smith and Alan

Shearer helped Leeds leapfrog Manchester United into top place for the final day of the season.

A 3-1 win over Everton on the final day at Goodison Park was enough for Leeds to capture their first league title in twelve years as Ferguson's reign of domination at the top of the Premier League was seemingly over.

Due to Alan Smith's form, he was integral to England's qualification campaign for the European Championships in 2004 and subsequent to Alan Shearer's signing at Elland Road and their form in the previous season; he managed to coax his teammate out of international retirement.

With Wayne Rooney in a playmaker role behind Shearer and Smith, England romped through the group stages, simply outscoring their opponents as the Leeds pairing netted seven between them in the groups. England sauntered through an explosive Group B with nine points, beating the likes of France, Switzerland and Croatia handsomely, scoring twelve goals in the process, whilst conceding eight.

Portugal were England's quarter final opponents and without the suspended Wayne Rooney, Alan Shearer had to wait for extra time to net his winning goal in the 112th minute in a comparatively subdued 1-0 win, matched up with England's previous three encounters in the tournament. Alan Smith would score in a semi-final date with Czech Republic in a 3-0 win whilst all three of the England forwards netted in the final against Greece, a 4-2 win which solidified England's place at the top of European football. England struck twenty-one times in six matches—the 38 years of hurt were officially over.

Whilst Shearer re-affirmed his international retirement after the tournament, leaving a sufficient partnership between Smith and Rooney, the former went onto bigger and better things, claiming the 2010 FIFA World Cup in his international swansong. In that tournament the Leeds forward scored his 53rd international goal in a 2-0 final win over Italy, scoring six in the tournament and becoming England's top goalscorer not just in World Cup history and in the tournament in Germany but of all-time, pipping Sir Bobby Charlton's record by four goals.

After the European Championships in Portugal, Smith helped Leeds to four more league titles as the class of 2004 had all retired and had been replaced by the new generation in 2014. The European final that David O'Leary promised under his tenure did come true though.

In 2007, after winning successive league titles as well as their third FA Cup under David O'Leary, he guided them to the Champions League final against A.C. Milan. However, the likes of Kaka and Filippo Inzaghi would prove too strong for the West Yorkshire club on this night and despite an Alan Smith goal, Leeds United bowed out of the final, losing 2-1.

They would participate in the knockout stages under David O'Leary from 2001 to his retirement in 2012 without fail but would never win a European crown, or reach another final. It became the prize that had eluded the Irishman and Leeds, both in the seventies against Bayern Munich and in Athens, against A.C. Milan in 2007.

16

Argentine Dominance

Lionel Messi, at the time of writing, currently houses four FIFA Ballon d'Or accolades in his trophy cabinet, more than any other player in the history of the game. Since the award was merged with the FIFA World Player of the Year award in 2009, the Barcelona talisman can now state he has more player of the year titles than the neighbourhood of Johan Cryuff, Michel Platini and Marco van Basten who have all collected three of the award.

Ronaldo holds three FIFA World Player of the Year awards (1996, 1997 and 2002) along with two Ballon d'Or awards in those years, landing him on five. You can expect Lionel Messi to equal and subsequently better that record in the forthcoming years.

Messi has done it all at his only club, Barcelona, collecting Champions League medals in 2006, 2009 and 2011—all over English opposition with multiple La Liga trophies and worldwide accolades such as the FIFA Club World Cup and the UEFA Super Cup. Domestically, Barca have dominated Spain in the past few years under the management of Guardiola and Vilanova, adding the Copa del Rey and the Spanish Super Cup to Messi's collection.

Internationally, he has appeared in a Copa America final, losing 3-0 to Brazil in 2007—but that's exactly where the hole in Lionel Messi's trophy cabinet is; the international silverware. Two FIFA World Cup quarter final defeats to Germany along with multiple disappointments with Argentina in the Copa America has left Messi without a single piece of international silverware.

Of course, there is plenty of time for the diminutive playmaker to rectify this and at the age of 26, time is on his side. After obliterating the record for goals in a Champions League season in 2011-12, he soon after finished that same season with seventy-three goals, leaving the likes of Atletico Madrid's Falcao and Real Madrid's Cristiano Ronaldo for dust both in terms of goals and domestic silverware.

Subsequently, in November, he defeated Pele's record of 75 goals in a calendar year with only one man in his sights — Gerd Muller. After netting his 91st and last goal of 2012 against Real Valladolid, Messi surpassed Muller's all-time record of eighty-five by six goals.

Messi was immortalised in both Barcelona and footballing folklore as one of, if not, the best player to have ever played the sport. Of course, players from different timeframes such as Pele, Diego Maradona, Zinedine Zidane amongst others that I have mentioned in this book can all compete for the 'best footballer ever' compliment.

However, the whole nature of football has changed since Pele won his first FIFA World Cup at the age of 17 in 1958, from Maradona's World Cup winning side in 1986 to Zidane's infamous headbutt in 2006 to quell a second French title at the World Cup. The game has changed not only in its many rules but tactically as well. Many names have come and gone in the present day sport, Messi is engaged with a battle against Cristiano Ronaldo for the best player on the planet.

One of the problems for the Argentine in this particular battle is that he's only proven himself in

Spain. It's obvious for the entire world to see that Messi will never leave Barcelona, he left Argentina at a very young age to play for the club as a child. Cristiano Ronaldo has proven himself in both England and Spain—two of the most competitive leagues in the world, whilst Messi has stuck at one club, gaining undoubted success.

The greats such as Zidane earned plaudits in multiple countries, as did Diego Maradona. In fact, Maradona breached the European stage with Napoli and Barcelona, unlike Pele, who he often competes with, according to pundits and supporters, in terms of gauging the best player ever to play football. Former pundit and commentator for *Sky Sports*, Andy Gray once remarked in 2010 that "Messi would struggle on a cold night at the Britannia Stadium" if he joined the Premier League.

But what if he wasn't playing right now? What if Lionel Messi debuted in the late seventies, breaking into the same achieving squad as fellow compatriot and Argentine legend, Diego Maradona? Could he add international silverware to his CV as well as the club accolades that he has achieved with Barcelona?

The Estadio Monumental in Buenos Aries on June 6th, 1978 housed a shade over 70,000 people to see Argentina's capitulation in their own backyard at a FIFA World Cup group stage match against France. A couple of goals from Michel Platini helped the French to a 2-0 win over the Argentine and subsequently eliminated them from the tournament in only the second match of Argentina's tournament.

A 3-2 loss to Hungary in the previous match meant a win was needed against France to keep their dreams of a first FIFA World Cup title alive. A flat 0-0 draw against Italy in the final group game spelled the end of Argentina in the tournament, gaining only one point from three games and becoming the first side to bow out at the first round whilst hosting the tournament.

After the humiliation in the tournament, which would ultimately be won by Italy, an intense scouting regime took up the Argentine national side programme and just seven short months later later it spat out Lionel Messi, a thirteen year-old from the province of Santa Fe.

The young Argentine, who was only four-foot-eleven, at the time was heralded as the next best thing for the sport and the country alongside Diego Maradona who debuted for the national team two years previously in 1977.

After scoring twenty-eight goals in a junior game, Messi was successfully scouted for River Plate and made his debut in a 3-0 win over Newell's Old Boys, where he got the third and final goal as a substitute.

River Plate won the Metropolitano Championship as well as the Nacional Championship in an Argentine domestic double with Messi as their kingpin in midfield. Although the Argentine was assigned to an attacking midfield role in a 4-4-1-1 formation, he ventured forward frequently, joining the attack and consequently scoring 47 times in 36 games for the Argentine outfit. European clubs were soon on the phone for the best product since sliced bread.

After a handful of games in the 1980 season for River Plate which featured two hat-tricks from Messi and four further goals, the man who scouted him just fourteen months previously paid for his plane ticket to the Malpensa Airport in Milan, Italy in April 1980.

From there, Messi was swiftly transported to Naples

where in the space of two weeks he competed in three reserve team matches for Napoli, in a trial run for the Serie A outfit.

Messi declared in a 1997 interview with Marca, "I wasn't ready for the first game, we played Siena I think and after fifty or so minutes I got pulled off the bench to play in the reserves match. I mean, just seventy-two hours earlier I'd scored for River Plate in a league match and here I was in a foreign country where nobody spoke a word of my language, I didn't think I could adjust to the cold conditions in March."

Messi scored two goals in fifteen minutes before he was hauled off the pitch. The Argentine recounted in the same interview that he was whisked away by the first team manager, Rino Marchesi, and was summoned to get some rest because he would be playing in the all-important cup semi-final for the reserve side the following day. The talent was identified immediately, Napoli were about to receive one of the best footballing prospects the world had ever seen except nobody knew it yet.

Twenty hours later, Messi scored a further five goals in a story that was even picked up by the national newspapers throughout Italy. Napoli's reserve side beat Palermo's 7-0 in a match which, the Italian newspapers and mainstream media, heralded Lionel Messi a future Italian international.

It came with great disappointment, three months later, that Napoli labelled the announcement regarding Messi's signing of "the Argentine wonderkid", who had turned fifteen just mere weeks prior to the press conference. He was offloaded to the press conference where Napoli paraded him around the small room like a trophy.

A month or so later, Messi was becoming the youngest ever player to play in the Serie A, at fourteen years and two months. Although Messi was used primarily for reserve matches and runouts in the 'B' team which were further down the divisional ladder in Italy, he got a taste of Serie A action.

Netting twelve times in seventeen matches would have been impressive by anybody's standards but by a fourteen year old who simply waltzed through the famous Juventus line-up before beating Dino Zoff all ends up to secure a 2-1 win in Turin, he had become an overnight success in Italy.

He turned out for some of the younger Argentine sides throughout that season, including the under-21's for a match in which he scored four times against Bolivian opponents. It seemed as though Messi was primed for the big leagues.

A hat-trick in a senior Coppa Italia quarter-final tie against Cagliari sent the Italian media into a frenzied state. Messi scored an impressive sixty-two times in almost as many matches upon his departure in 1983 with his biggest accolade of them all coming as a winning member of the Napoli side who toppled Juventus by a matter of five goals in the 1981-82 season.

Messi was snapped up by Hamburg for an astounding six million pounds, breaking compatriot, Diego Maradona's record when he was purchased by Barcelona the previous year. Hamburg almost had money to burn after their European Cup triumph over Juventus in 1983.

At the age of 16, Messi would have broken the record set by Pele for being the youngest goalscorer at a FIFA World Cup by a full year and a half but coach Cesar

Luis Menotti cruelly left Lionel Messi out who had just come off the back of a Serie A title win with Napoli and was reportedly hungry for success and a runout in the national side. Menotti replied with a simple rebuttal "you have to earn a place in the national side by proving your technique and strength, not by scoring goals against under-par Italian teams".

A year older and wiser, Lionel Messi netted twice in his debut for Hamburg against Stuttgart in the opening day of the 1983-84 Bundesliga and would make his first senior appearance for the national side in a Copa America match against Ecuador in August of the same year. In November 1983, Messi scored his first national side goal in a friendly with Sweden, his third appearance.

By that point in time, he'd already notched up fifteen goals for Hamburg and fired them into the latter stages of the European Cup and to the top of the Bundesliga. Eight goals in Argentina's qualification campaign for the 1986 FIFA World Cup was integral to their qualification in the earlier part of 1984, meanwhile, Messi was announcing himself on the world stage in Germany.

Two goals away at Bayern Munich confirmed the Bundesliga title, earlier than ever before, on March 17th, 1984 with a 3-0 win as Hamburg lost just once throughout the domestic season. In European competition, Hamburg were steamrolling their opponents into submission from the likes of Dinamo Bucharest and Athletic Bilbao in the opening rounds to Benfica in the quarter finals. After a 3-0 aggregate win over the Portuguese outfit the subsequent semi-final threw up Roma and with the possibility of facing European giants, Liverpool in the final, Lionel Messi was particularly fired up after scoring all three against Benfica in the quarter final ties.

Four further goals in two matches against the Italian side Roma, who Messi had a great record against, fired Hamburg into a third European Cup final in five seasons. Inside the Olympic Stadium in Rome for the European Cup final against Liverpool, whoever didn't know a certain seventeen year old Argentinian footballer did after the final.

Messi's two goals helped sink Liverpool, 3-2 after extra time in Rome as Hamburg sealed a second European Cup in as many years. The double reduced the teenager to tears as he ran through the stadium clutching at his prized possession—the European Cup. Two years later, he'd be lifting another one of football's greatest trophies.

Successive Bundesliga titles and a further dozen international goals had built Lionel Messi up towards the 1986 FIFA World Cup where, after the semi-final disappointment in 1982, Argentina were determined to prevail in Mexico and were amongst the favourites which included West Germany and Brazil.

The nineteen year old, turning twenty, started the opening group match alongside Diego Maradona and Jorge Valdano up front for Argentina against South Korea. A couple of goals for Messi proved the difference in a 3-1 win. Another two goals in the matches against Italy and Bulgaria respectively had Messi prevailing over Maradona in the goalscoring charts by a single goal. Messi was winning that particular battle 4-3, but the same scoreline was replicated in their dramatic second round win over Uruguay after notching up a 100% record in the group stages.

Maradona had proven superior over the younger Messi against Uruguay, striking a hat-trick past their fellow South American opponents but up next were a different assortment of players—the English which included talisman Gary Lineker who headed the tournament's scoring chart.

An early second half goal from the Everton striker had Argentina reeling shortly after the half-time break but the combination between Valdano and Messi was proving unstoppable for the best of defences, never mind England's. Valdano teed Messi's first and second strikes up as Argentina would race into an unassailable 4-1 lead, the 19-year old netting all four.

With eight strikes on the board for the tournament, Messi had turned twenty by the time semi-final opponents Belgium came a knocking in Mexico City. All three forwards netted in a 5-0 demolition of another European nation and with West Germany forthcoming, many had Argentina down as their new tournament favourites.

Messi clinched the golden boot with two goals in the final, racing to an almost record eleven goals for the tournament as Maradona provided the other two goals in a damning display for the West Germans, their worst FIFA World Cup defeat, a 4-0 destruction in the Mexican capital.

Argentina had finally secured their first FIFA World Cup and a year later, Lionel Messi lifted his first Copa America, Argentina's first since 1959. By which time, Messi was winning yet another Bundesliga title with Hamburg.

Messi didn't relent in his final three years at Hamburg as the German club only failed to win the Bundesliga once (in 1989) in the eight seasons that the Argentina graced the club, with a second European Cup title coming in 1988.

This time, Hamburg's supporters enjoyed it a little bit more than their previous two European titles as they toppled compatriots and enemies, Bayern Munich, with the help of course from a Lionel Messi hat-trick in the first ever all-German European Cup final. After a trophyless season in 1989, a domestic double in 1990 prepared Messi for his second FIFA World Cup tournament, at the age of 23.

He was only nearing his prime and prior to the tournament in Italy, Messi would secretly sign a contract away from Hamburg, to Nottingham Forest, much to the persuasion of Brian Clough and the anguish of the Hamburg fans. Messi was leaving behind his 312 goals in eight seasons for German club, Hamburg for Nottingham Forest—and he was only just reaching his 24th birthday. There was a lot more to come from the Argentine wonderkid.

Lionel Messi clinched Argentina's place at the top of Group B almost single-handedly. The diminutive forward scored six of Argentina's seven goals in the group stages as they wrapped up a knockout stage berth with a 4-0 win over Romania in the final group match which featured another Messi hat-trick whilst Maradona netted the other.

Wins over the likes of Colombia, England and West Germany lead Argentina to face Brazil, a formidable World Cup opponent, in the final in Rome. At this stage, Lionel Messi was residing high and mighty at the top of the goalscoring ranks with nine goals. The recently turned 24-year old would score the winner in a dull 1-0 win over the Brazilians as Argentina claimed successive FIFA World Cup triumphs, the first side since Brazil (1958 and 1962) to do so.

It would become the same story four years later in the United States as Lionel Messi and Diego Maradona equalled Pele's record of FIFA World Cup titles of three, with a further seven goals for Messi, who took his international account to seventy-two. Brazil were once again the victims of a final defeat, being thrashed 4-1 in Pasadena's Rose Bowl as Argentina claimed a third successive World Cup crown—a first.

At that point in time, Lionel Messi had long outgrown Nottingham Forest. 47 goals in 45 matches in his only season in Nottingham was enough for Alex Ferguson to reward him with an eleven million pound deal to Old Trafford in the summer of 1991.

At Forest he helped the Midlands club clinch second place in the First Division by a hair from Arsenal and a League Cup triumph over Liverpool as he started planning life as a Manchester United player. Ferguson's plan from the start of the 1991-92 season was evident as the Cup Winners' Cup champions looked for the link between young Welsh winger, Ryan Giggs and Lionel Messi.

Six league titles, almost two hundred goals, four FA Cup titles and another two UEFA Champions League crowns in 1995 and 1997 had Lionel Messi prepared sufficiently to go out of international football on a high as he looked to retire from the Argentine national squad at the age of 32 at the end of the 1998 FIFA World Cup tournament in France.

Five more goals in his FIFA World Cup account was enough for Messi to lead Argentina out into a Paris final with Brazil, for the third successive tournament. The pre-match hype was surrounding Brazilian, Ronaldo who could pip Messi to the golden boot, which would be a first since 1982, and subsequently win Brazil's first World Cup in twenty-eight years.

The pair exchanged four goals and the match went into a penalty shootout, the first World Cup final to do so. Messi was confirmed as the golden boot winner for the fourth tournament in succession, scoring his sixth and seventh goals whilst Ronaldo could only manage to add a sixth to his tally.

Ronaldo would have the last laugh as he converted his penalty whilst Messi missed his kick in the shootout, allowing Cafu to seal Brazil's fourth FIFA World Cup triumph in a 4-3 shootout win, surpassing Italy and Argentina's record of three.

Messi would retire from football altogether five summers later in 2003 at the age of 36, ending his twelve-year tenure at Manchester United, not before he added another UEFA Champions League in 2002, with a hat-trick against Real Madrid in the final. Messi was hailed as Sir Alex Ferguson's "greatest ever player" in a poll held on Manchester United's official website upon the manager's retirement in 2013.

The Argentine added two more Premier League winning medals and reached a tally of 1,142 goals in his professional career from 1,304 appearances—the best goal return known in the history of the professional game. Messi will be forever marked as one of the most decorated players in the sport, winning eighteen league titles across four countries. In 2002, he also became one of a band of players in the neighbourhood of Alessandro Costacurta and Paolo Maldini to win five UEFA Champions League winners' medals.

He ranks alongside Pele and Diego Maradona as the only three players to win three FIFA World Cup medals and has attained sixteen domestic cup accolades for four of the five clubs he turned out for along with two Copa America titles in 1987 and 1995.

Messi still holds the record of FIFA World Cup goals, scoring thirty-four goals in twenty-eight World Cup games as he eclipsed Gerd Muller's record of fourteen rather comprehensively. Having appeared as an ever-present at four successive FIFA World Cups for Argentina, he shades the all-time appearance record at the World Cup too, appearing in three more matches than Germany's Lothar Matthaus.

Pele named him on the FIFA 100 shortlist, the list of greatest living players in the world of sport. To this day, Messi remains as the only player to win three successive Ballon d'Or trophies (1987, 1988 and 1989) and holds the record for winning the accolade six times, with further titles in 1991, 1994 and 1995.

17

Bloemfontein Ghost Goal

On the 27th of June, 2010, Fabio Capello's England took on Germany in the second round of the FIFA World Cup in Bloemfontein, South Africa. For the first time in a decade, the two nations would lock horns at a major tournament but, unfortunately for England, Germany would gain revenge for their loss in Belgium at the 2000 European Championships.

Thomas Muller struck twice in the match and announced himself to the world with five goals in the tournament sharing the top of the goalscoring chart in the company of Diego Forlan, David Villa and Wesley Sneijder. Goals from the experienced pair of Miroslav Klose and Lukas Podolski along with Muller's efforts were enough to palm off England 4-1 and progress to the quarter finals, inflicting England's worst defeat at a major tournament.

Argentina would become Germany's next victims in their following outing as they were humiliated 4-0 in the quarter finals. Subsequently, the Germans went down 1-0 to eventual winners, Spain in the semi-finals whilst the English team were already sunning themselves on holiday with a bitter taste in their mouth.

That bitter taste was courtesy of the match officials for the second round match in the World Cup. Two goals from Klose and Podolski had carved England open in already poor tournament for Capello's men but were rejuvenated when a soft Matthew Upson header regained English hope.

After Upson's goal in the 37th minute, England were buoyed by the hope of a possible comeback and almost instantly Frank Lampard had the ball, twenty-five yards out from Manuel Neuer's goalposts.

The Chelsea midfielder, who holds the record for most shots on goal without scoring at a FIFA World Cup, thought he'd finally broke his scoring duck. A volley which was lofted over the-then Schalke goalkeeper clipped the underside of the crossbar and bounced a full foot-and-a-half over the immaculately painted German goal line.

BBC commentators Steve Wilson and Mark Lawrenson were almost complimenting the strike until the Uruguayan officials and German players continued with the game.

Every England supporter both inside the stadium and in various venues watching the match were in total disbelief as the match continued, despite the fact that England should have pulled themselves level in the game.

At that point in the match, the English would have the initiative and would have been able to strike whilst the iron was hot but instead were made to pay a huge price for the erroneous officials—FIFA World Cup elimination and their worst ever result at a major tournament.

Muller's second half goals scored on swift counter attacks were the product of desperate England attacks as they searched for an equaliser to keep themselves in the World Cup. It marked a sad day for English football as they crashed out at the last sixteen stage for the first time in twelve years.

Two years later, the endless calls for goal line technology in the sport, which had fallen behind the likes of Tennis and Cricket who both implemented such systems as HawkEye into the game, were finally answered as Sepp Blatter approved of the technology.

The Swiss FIFA President green lit trial runs at the 2012 FIFA Club World Cup and the Confederations Cup in 2013 before announcing that all FIFA tournaments from the 2014 World Cup onwards would use the goal line technology. Premier League chief executive, Richard Scudamore subsequently announced plans to use British goal line technology system HawkEye from the 2013-14 season onwards as the movement gathered pace.

England fans can only wonder what if Frank Lampard's goal in the FIFA World Cup counted against Germany. Could they have managed to progress into the quarter finals and gone onto win the tournament, or would they have faltered against Germany anyway?

The ball spouted out to Frank Lampard, in the 39th minute, who hit the ball first time as it rose. The English midfielder's effort lofted over Manuel Neuer, crossing the line after it clipped the underside of the crossbar and before the German goalkeeper gobbled the ball up into his chest, the Uruguayan referee ruled in favour of England. They had drawn level just before half-time.

Whilst the half-time break allowed the Germans some respite, England were on a high after two quickfire goals at the end of the half and looked capable to take the game by the scruff of the neck and qualify for the quarter finals.

The second half was almost a war of attrition, built

upon the two nations' fear of making a mistake but the match would not have to be decided on such a circumstance. Alternatively, a momentary flick of a right boot combined with a misdirected flailing right glove would pluck England out of the last sixteen, dropping them into the final eight of the FIFA World Cup to meet Argentina.

A Wayne Rooney back heel in the 67th minute was enough to beat both Manuel Neuer and Germany on a sunny day in the climbs of Bloemfontein as England marched onto meet Argentina six days later in Cape Town following the 3-2 victory.

The piece of officiating in the previous round was the flick of the switch that England needed to get back on track in the tournament as Wayne Rooney and Jermain Defoe seemed to simply click as a partnership up front for the English against Argentina in the quarter final. The Manchester United forward would score a double as he sunk Lionel Messi's Argentina to progress to a first World Cup semi-final for the first time in two decades since the 1990 penalty shootout disappointment against West Germany.

The pressure from the media that had disintegrated from a poor group stage campaign had returned on the eve of the semi-final against Spain in anticipation and excitement for the big occasion ahead. The English supporters were already dreaming of a second World Cup final but there was the biggest of obstacles in their way—the reigning European champions and tournament favourites Spain.

Carlos Puyol headed the Spanish into a very early lead in Durban and by half-time, the pundits inside the ITV studio were lamenting the English performance, not highlighting the technique and pure skill in which

Spain were pulling England around the pitch.

Moments into the second half, Wayne Rooney scored yet another invaluable goal, scoring a long-distance equaliser to reinvigorate an apparently "lacklustre" English performance. The winning goal fell to the man that the journalists loved to write about, the pundits loved to discuss and that supporters got infuriated about, because of his lack of goals — Emile Heskey.

The Aston Villa forward, who had scored two goals all season, stepped up when England needed him most, scoring an unbelievable goal which ricocheted off the side of his neck which subsequently trickled into an empty Spanish net. The timing of the goal couldn't have been better either as Heskey saved his first and final positive moment at that tournament until the 118th minute so the Spanish couldn't launch a response in the final couple of minutes in the extra time period.

The English partied through the course of the night in Durban as in four nights' time they would be colliding with the roughhouses of the Netherlands, unfortunately that was all too literal for one Englishman in the final on that night. The Dutch were looking for their first World Cup in their third appearance at a final whilst England were staring at a match they had only competed in once before — in 1966 when a Geoff Hurst hat-trick saw off West Germany at Wembley Stadium.

The pairing of Mark van Bommel and Nigel de Jong were doing a splendid job of putting out fires in the middle of the park in the Soccer City stadium come the day of the final as their robust challenges were met with the ignorance from Italian referee Nicola Rizzoli. Holland had pushed, pulled and grabbed their way to a third World Cup final, a stark contrast from the "Total Football" philosophy led by former international Johan Cryuff during the seventies—where the Netherlands made their other two appearances at a World Cup final.

One man felt the brunt of the opposition midfield all too well as midway through the opening half of the contest, Frank Lampard was sent clattering to the floor following a less than impressive tackle from Nigel de Jong. The Manchester City midfielder threw the studs of his boot into the sternum of Frank Lampard, fracturing the sternal bone in the process which knocked Frank Lampard out of the final and almost unconscious.

The Chelsea midfielder was carried from the pitch and, according to the man himself in an interview, he was lucky to survive, "The World Cup final was rough, I woke up in a hospital in Johannesburg that night and lost all memory of the incident, it was only until I was told by the doctors what happened, I was devastated."

"I wasn't devastated by the injury, yes I was lucky in some respects to be able to play football in the second half of the next season, but the result devastated me. I was inconsolable when the nurses and my family told me we had lost 2-0 to the Dutch. Of course, I've watched many of the highlights from the match and I don't hold a grudge against Nigel, he only had eyes for the ball. I was more upset by our performance."

Without the instrumental Frank Lampard, England flopped to a second half defeat as Holland were victorious in the FIFA World Cup final at the third time of asking. The Chelsea midfielder and the whole of the English support and coaching staff remain bemused to this day at how Nigel de Jong managed to stay on the pitch following the tackle.

He was cautioned for the dangerous tackle, and if that wasn't galling enough, he scored one of the two goals that helped Holland to the title in South Africa.

For his part in the final, Nigel de Jong was exiled by Manchester City manager, Roberto Mancini just eighteen months into his contract for his actions both in the match and afterwards at the club's training facilities. Mancini reported of an obvious rift between the English contingent in the camp and Nigel de Jong along with a few of the coaching staff and "had no other option but to sell Nigel" the Italian claimed in a pre-season interview.

De Jong would be banished from England, snapped up a cut-price by Juventus for six and a half million pounds as Frank Lampard attempted a miraculous recovery. The Chelsea midfielder never truly recovered to his pre-tournament footballing ability as he admitted to in an in-depth interview with Piers Morgan on his Life Stories ITV talk show.

Lampard stated in the interview, "it was the turning point of my career, I returned initially from the injury about eight months later in February. Carlo Ancelotti, our new manager at the time, was very cautious about the whole situation and of course, I thought I could play before Christmas which I blatantly wasn't up to."

He would recall such moments in the famous interview following the World Cup like his first match back, a UEFA Champions League second round tie with none other than Juventus. "Going into the match, I wasn't sure of my selection so I wasn't getting emotional or anything about being Nigel's opponent," Frank claimed, "and even when I discovered that I was picked for the match in Italy, I felt no emotion but sheer happiness that I had broken into the team again. I was glad to be playing football again after an injury like the one I sustained."

The Chelsea midfielder was showing great signs of recovery following the Christmas period according the staff and by other members of the squad. He lined up against his former foe, Nigel de Jong in Turin on that February evening and ultimately got the better of him.

Lampard recounted the events of the match in numerous interviews since, "as soon as I got the ball for the first time, I felt the crowd's eyes burning into my back, the insults and the abuse I was receiving from the Juventus fans. We won the game 2-1 because of my winning goal I'd like to think but I didn't feel like a winner after the match."

"Afterwards I felt shocked by the reaction from the home supporters but that aside the pain that had left me for a few weeks in my chest was back. A few days later and I'm being checked into the physio's room and he was talking to me, telling me I was lucky for even being able to get through the ninety minutes." Lampard would complete a further nine matches in his career, scoring just one more as Chelsea were left with a void in the midfield upon his retirement in 2012—two years after the initial injury.

There was no doubt in anybody's mind to this day that the injury suffered at the FIFA World Cup dramatically cut short a wonderful playing career. The Chelsea midfielder, who now coaches the youth set-up at Stamford Bridge was magnanimous in his description of Nigel de Jong in meetings with the press since the incident in the final.

Lampard labelled the Dutch midfielder a superb athlete and a great reader of the game. The former

Chelsea man can also take solace from the event which took place after his first match back from injury in Turin, confronting Nigel de Jong whilst on the pitch.

"I walked up to Nigel after the game, congratulated him on a good, spirited match and he apologised for the supporters during the match and for the tackle the previous summer at the World Cup. I told him, 'Don't worry about that, mate, it's a contact sport, I've seen the replays enough times to know you didn't mean to injure me.' And after that moment we've kept in contact."

Whilst Lampard would witness the fall in stature of Chelsea down the Premier League from their title win in 2010 to eighth place in 2013, he would mastermind the youth squad to the FA Youth Cup in 2015 which he claimed was both his best experience and achievement in football.

Alternatively, Nigel de Jong raked home four Serie A titles for Juventus whilst winning the elusive UEFA Champions League in 2012 after a penalty shootout win over Bayern Munich at the Allianz Arena. He was made captain for Holland in his final swansong tournament as an international but the Dutch were eliminated in the quarter finals by Italy at the 2016 European Championships. He retired in 2019 with a collection of winners' medals, trophies and accolades at both club and international level.

18

Bayern's Famous Treble

On the 26th of May, 1999 one of the latest and greatest comebacks of European footballing history took place in the Nou Camp, Barcelona. The UEFA Champions League final concluded the 1998-99 European football calendar as Bayern Munich competed with Manchester United for the evidence of a treble-winning season as the trophy's ribbons were being prepared inside the stadium during the dramatic contest.

Of course, on the journey down the stadium's elevator, the ribbons of Bayern Munich would be forced into a dramatic transformation thanks to two injury time goals from Teddy Sheringham and Ole Gunnar Solskjaer which overturned an advantage created almost two hours earlier in the evening from a Mario Basler free-kick. It would be Peter Schmeichel, sentimental captain for the evening in his last match for United because of Roy Keane's suspension, collecting the famous trophy instead of Bayern captain and fellow goalkeeper Oliver Kahn because of three crucial injury time minutes which shaped the entire season and forthcoming seasons for both clubs.

Without the Champions League crown, Manchester United would only be celebrating their third domestic double in six years, a commonplace achievement in such a decade of dominance for Sir Alex Ferguson and United.

The unprecedented treble included shading the

Premier League title by a point from Arsenal before defeating Newcastle United in the penultimate Wembley FA Cup final just a couple of days before the Champions League showdown at the Nou Camp. For Bayern, however, a fifteen-point victory in the Bundesliga was the high point of their season after two final defeats to United and to Werder Bremen in the DFB-Pokal, Germany's primary domestic cup competition, in a penalty shootout defeat.

So after achieving just one piece of silverware in what could have been so different for the German club, they set themselves the target of achieving that fourth triumph at Europe's top table. Their first Champions League crown came two years after the heartbreak in Barcelona as they pipped Valencia to the European title in 2001, decades after trio of titles courtesy of the golden generation which consisted of Gerd Muller and the like from 1974 to 1976.

Manchester United's dominance saw them claim a third Champions League crown in 2008, pipping Chelsea to Europe's top club competition on penalties thanks, in part, to a John Terry slip during the shootout. Two more final defeats to Barcelona in 2009 and 2011 left Sir Alex Ferguson as one of the more decorated managers in Champions League history upon his retirement in 2013.

There was another retirement in 2013, as Jupp Heynckes ended his tenure at Bayern Munich with the holy grail of Champions League heading to Munich for the first time in twelve years. It was Heynckes' second European title, capturing his first as a manager in 1998 with Real Madrid. Bayern's fifth Champions League title came in the first all-German final in 2013, beating compatriots Borussia Dortmund at Wembley with a late winning goal of their own courtesy of Arjen Robben a minute from time to sink their German enemies.

What could have changed in both Bayern Munich and Manchester United's history if Bayern lifted the Champions League in 1999 instead of the English club?

The Manchester United half of the packed-out Nou Camp rose to its feet as the clock ticked over to stoppage time, with a couple of minutes allocated. United were attempting to pry their club out of the shell that they had played in throughout the opening ninety minutes of normal time, in order to claim their second European Cup crown. However, an over-hit corner from David Beckham curled harmlessly out for a Bayern goal kick and the German club held out for the allotted three minutes of injury time to claim their fourth UEFA Champions League crown. It was a first for Bayern for twenty-three years since a solitary Franz Roth goal in the 1976 European Cup final helped the German club to a third successive title in the tournament, beating French side Saint-Etienne at Hampden Park in Glasgow.

Manchester United returned for the 1999-2000 Premier League season away at Everton without the big name signing that was promised from Alex Ferguson. Instead, Bayern Munich announced the signing of Ruud van Nistelrooy forty-seven days after their European triumph for seventeen million pounds in what *Sky Sports* claimed would create a dream frontline which already contained Carsten Jancker and Mario Basler.

Bayern began their Bundesliga season with thirteen successive victories whilst Manchester United were trailing Arsenal and Leeds United by five points in third place by the end of November. Ferguson didn't receive the knighthood which seemed forthcoming on the eve of the Champions League final some six months ago.

A third double-winning season wasn't enough for the Manchester United fans it seemed and sure enough, after Christmas, Ferguson's side crashed out of the FA Cup at the fourth round stage thanks to a shocking 1-0 home loss to Nottingham Forest which saw the cynics which were in hiding half a year later emerge from the terraces.

United would only tie up second place on the final day of the season after a 2-0 win away at Wimbledon which kept Liverpool at bay in third place. United ultimately lost out on a second successive Premier League title to Arsenal by a huge nine points, their biggest losing margin in the Premier League era and the most they had been off the pace since 1991.

Arsenal were only deprived of their first ever UEFA Champions League in the final in May 2000 after losing 3-0 to Bayern Munich, where a hat-trick from Carsten Jancker settled a fifth Champions League crown for the German side. To add the cherry onto the already depressing Manchester United cake, Arsenal stole two transfer targets from under their nose in preparation of the 2000-01 season when both Patrick Kluivert and Juan Sebastian Veron chose Highbury over Old Trafford for a combined fee of forty-eight million from Barcelona and Lazio respectively.

This left slim pickings for an underachieving Manchester United side as Ferguson plumped for Emile Heskey after losing out on Ronaldinho to Paris Saint-Germain to lead their frontline alongside Dwight

Yorke, Andy Cole and Ole Gunnar Solskjaer after Teddy Sheringham's return to White Hart Lane in February 2001. Heskey's return of nine goals in fifty-one appearances up until the end of the 2001-02 wasn't a desirable statistic inside Old Trafford after two more trophyless seasons.

Ferguson was forced to keep faith in Emile Heskey through injuries to Yorke and Cole whilst United's finances were dwindling. Heskey wasn't selected for the 2002 FIFA World Cup, with Blackburn's Matt Jansen taking his place as part of the England squad in a disappointing campaign where Sven-Goran Eriksson's side crashed out to Denmark in the second round.

The Germans and the Dutch were trading the international honours at the turn of the century thanks to the two best goalscorers in world football—Jancker and Van Nistelrooy who had restored Bayern's dominance in Europe through two more Champions League crowns in 2001 and 2002, becoming only the second club in European Cup and Champions League history to win the tournament four times in succession.

The aforementioned Carsten Jancker was the top goalscorer in the European Championships in 2000 as he dragged an under-strengthened German side through to a final to face Italy. A hat-trick in the opener against Romania coupled with the decisive strikes against England and Portugal left Germany qualified for the quarter finals holding the only 100% record in the tournament.

A double for Jancker sunk Turkey in the quarter finals in a 4-0 hammering. Furthermore, he scored in the penalty shootout of a drab semi-final against nine-man France which finished 0-0. Jancker netted in a shootout which was won by the Germans 4-3.

Jancker struck twice in the final, netting nine of his nation's eleven goals at the tournament, his final two goals came in the 2-1 win over Italy which was concluded thanks to Jancker's 117th minute golden goal winner in extra time at Rotterdam's De Kuip stadium.

The inclusion of Ruud van Nistelrooy in the Dutch qualifying campaign for the 2002 FIFA World Cup allowed Holland to qualify for an eighth successive major tournament, the last failure being the 1986 FIFA World Cuo. The Bayern forward netted five goals in three qualifying matches to help them leapfrog Ireland to qualify for the tournament in the Far East. Meanwhile, Germany were sauntering to yet another World Cup appearance after qualifying ahead of England, wrapping up the campaign with a 2-0 win over Eriksson's side in Berlin in September 2001.

Germany would meet Holland in the World Cup final where Van Nistelrooy's Dutch side prevailed in Japan to win their first FIFA World Cup tournament, defeating Jancker's Germany as the two Bayern Munich forwards shared eleven goals throughout the tournament.

Bayern surrendered their first Champions League title for the first time in five years in 2003 at the hands of Arsenal's first crown as Patrick Kluivert netted thirteen of Arsenal's goals in the campaign. Alternatively up north, Manchester United crashed out at the second round of group stages.

A 3-0 away defeat at the hands of Panathinaikos on the final day saw Lazio leapfrog United to qualify alongside Real Madrid. Alex Ferguson's response to a third successive third place finish in the Premier

League was to snap up Paolo di Canio from West Ham in August 2003, the thirty-five year old was viewed as a desperation buy and 'out of United's character' according to a Manchester United European Cup winner from 1968—Paddy Crerand.

A fifth successive Bundesliga crown for Bayern Munich was sealed in 2003 in part because of Ruud van Nistelrooy's thirty-one goals in thirty-four league appearances. A fee of forty-one million was enough to pluck the Dutchman from Germany, throwing him right into the lion's den of an opening day massacre in the English Premier League in August.

Fortunately for Ruud, the he was the instigator of the aforementioned massacre, scoring five goals in his first outing for Chelsea in the 2003-04 season, wrapping up a 7-0 victory at Stamford Bridge over Bolton Wanderers. The match would be Roman Abramovich's first in ownership of the club, who in turn granted a Premier League title at the first time of asking in 2004, along with successive accolades in 2005 and 2006. The holy grail of a further Champions League in was finally attained in 2006 with a 2-1 win over Manchester United. So what had changed for Manchester United and Alex Ferguson?

First of all, the new owners in Malcolm Glazer immediately fired Alex Ferguson in July 2005 after six successive years without a trophy, substituting him sufficiently with Arsene Wenger. Wenger brought with him the majority of the Arsenal coaching staff along with David Trezeguet and Didier Drogba in time for the 2005-06 season.

Wenger was walking a tightrope himself following an unsuccessful couple of seasons at Highbury after the highest of highs in the 2003 UEFA Champions League triumph, with just a League Cup in 2004 to show for all of his hard work.

The duo of Trezeguet and Drogba overshadowed the disappointing pair of Heskey and di Canio who were subsequently shipped out to Everton and Newcastle respectively. Alternatively, the incoming pair netted thirty-nine goals between them in Wenger's opening season as Manchester United gaffer.

United were only two points short of the Premier League pace in the 2005-06 season, ultimately losing out to Chelsea by the nearest of margins. Meanwhile in Germany, Bayern Munich claimed another Champions League crown with a win over Barcelona in the 2005 Istanbul final whilst they completed a double containing a seventh Bundesliga title in eight seasons, with a 2005 failure to Schalke being the only blemish in a rampant decade for Bayern.

At the conclusion of that decade, however, Bayern contained the flare of Cristiano Ronaldo who would collect three Champions League crowns from 2008 to 2013 as the German club overcame Real Madrid's long-standing record of nine titles in the famous trophy and prolonged Bayern's dominance. Whilst Ronaldo wouldn't gain any international honours in his Portuguese career, Germany as a footballing nation profited from Bayern's worldwide success, clinching three of five FIFA World Cups in the opening two decades of the millennium, triumphing in 2006, 2014 and 2018.

England would avenge their decades of hurt at a major tournament with a first

European Championships crown in 2012, beating Germany on the way to a final victory over Spain in Kiev.

The tyranny of Bayern throughout the opening decades of the 21st century wouldn't be ended by Manchester United as, under Wenger, they only claimed two Premier League titles in 2009 and 2014 as well as an FA Cup crown before his retirement in 2016.

The former Arsenal manager would bring a Champions League final to the Manchester United club in 2013 but were once again defeated by Bayern Munich at Wembley thanks to a double from Cristiano Ronaldo in an impressive 4-1 victory for the Germans, twelve years after the 1-0 victory for Bayern over United in the Nou Camp in 1999.

19

Aguer-d'oh

The climax of the 2011-12 Premier League season will never be matched for its drama, in terms of the race for the title. For the first time in a few decades, both Manchester clubs were competing for the top flight league title and the noisy neighbours in blue were in pole position to claim their third top flight title, their first in forty-four years.

Ever since the beginning of the 2008-09 season, Manchester City had re-announced themselves in the top pack of challengers for the Premier League alongside the usual suspects of Manchester United, Chelsea, Arsenal and Liverpool. Teams such as Aston Villa, Everton and Tottenham Hotspur were lurking with intent to break the constant mould of the top four of the Premier League, in order to be granted a spot in the UEFA Champions League.

Manchester City's new owner, Sheikh Mansour wasted little time in bringing big stars to the club as he reeled in Robinho on the transfer deadline day from Real Madrid for 32.5 million pounds.

Dimitar Berbatov was in City's sights too, but much like the previous decade and a half, the red half of Manchester beat them to it, signing Berbatov to rival the signature of Robinho on the same night.

Whilst City finished in the top half of the table in 2009, a lot of work needed to be done in time for the new season. Mark Hughes brought eight new players in for the 2009-10 season, with the most notable of which being the capture of Carlos Tevez after his two years at neighbouring club, Manchester United.

The short distance between clubs coupled with the blue billboard which advertised the former United forward in a City shirt shook the entire city for that season. United had the last laugh, even if they didn't win the league that year as they beat their rivals both home and away.

A Premier League classic halted City early on as a late Michael Owen goal sunk City as Manchester United powered to the league's summit early on, winning 4-3 at Old Trafford in September 2009. The return fixture needed an old head to put United on top in stoppage time too, when Paul Scholes headed United into a 1-0 win at the Etihad Stadium in the reverse fixture in April. Hughes was sacked prior to the League Cup semi-finals which were contested over two legs by the neighbours. Tevez scored three times in the two encounters in the semi-final to intensify the rivalry but ultimately United progressed on aggregate over the two legs and would go onto triumph in the tournament, beating Aston Villa in the final thanks to the free-scoring Wayne Rooney.

New manager, Roberto Mancini brought in only a couple of faces for the second half of the season which would prove to be a disappointing conclusion to an otherwise promising start. Falling out of both cup competitions, they had just fourth place in their sights in the league after Hughes' latter form of two wins in ten over the festive period saw City languishing in sixth place and a long way off the leading pack in terms of their points tally.

A late Peter Crouch goal at the Etihad Stadium in May would consign Manchester City with a place in the Europa League for the 2010-11 season as Tottenham Hotspur finished fourth in the table, three points ahead of City who occupied fifth place.

City would improve upon their points tally from the previous season and build their way to mount a serious challenge for the 2011-12 season after placing third. Mancini brought home their first piece of silverware in the top flight since winning the League Cup in 1976 after a 1-0 win in the FA Cup final over Stoke City which sealed Mancini's first trophy whilst wearing the scarf of City's around his neck.

Mancini added seven more names to City's ranks in a changing of the guard in the summer of 2011. The likes of Hart, Tevez, Kompany, De Jong, Kolarov, Balotelli, Dzeko, Milner, Silva and Toure would soon be joined by the names of Clichy, Nasri and Aguero.

Although their opening Champions League campaign ended in a miserable finish in the group stages, City enjoyed a great start to the season, topping the league by Christmas. The 23rd of October, 2011 will live long in the memory within the blue half of Manchester after a 6-1 humbling of their giant rivals in their own backyard proved to be one of the season's turning points.

There were a lot of twists and turns in this particular title race though. Two successive defeats to Blackburn Rovers and Newcastle United saw Manchester United trail their rivals by a substantial margin at the turn of the year. However, the long absence of Carlos Tevez coupled with the in-camp disputes between Mario Balotelli and manager, Roberto Mancini kept Sir Alex Ferguson's side in the title hunt.

After a 1-0 loss at Swansea City thanks to a Luke Moore header, Manchester United overtook Mancini's

City with ten matches remaining. Five points from their next four matches saw City lagging increasingly behind United as they sauntered into a seemingly unassailable lead at the top.

Loss at the DW Stadium as well as letting a two-goal lead slip at home to Everton for Ferguson's United had re-opened the title door for the blue half of Manchester, who had coasted through their final matches because the pressure was evidently off, according to Mancini who was already announcing United as the new champions.

A Vincent Kompany header to win the second Manchester derby in the league that season put another spin on the title race before the final day of the season, which contained a see-saw of emotions for the fans in blue packed into the Etihad Stadium on May 13th, 2012.

Wayne Rooney scored the only goal for United before half-time in what would become a 1-0 win for the Red Devils but Pablo Zabaleta replied with a collector's item of a goal to put City back on top as it stood before all four sides went into the half-time break in the two matches which dominated the attention of the final day of the season.

It seemed like the twists for the title race were over as Manchester City were beating relegation-threatened Queen's Park Rangers with ease at home but two second half goals from Jamie Mackie and Djibril Cisse had United fans celebrating at the Stadium of Light with less than twenty-five minutes remaining.

A red card for Joey Barton left City fans buoyant as they looked for two goals in the final twenty minutes at home to 17th placed Rangers who were looking for their own result to stay up.

However, news was swirling round the away end that Bolton Wanderers had caved in, conceding a second half penalty which would kill all dreams off of another season in the top flight in their run which had lasted over a decade, as they were held 2-2 by Stoke City at the Britannia Stadium.

An Edin Dzeko equaliser in the second minute of injury time revitalised the frustrated City fans who thought they had blown their chance at a third English top flight crown, a first since 1968. City fans were urging the swarm of blue up the pitch as Manchester United concluded their match as champions, beating Sunderland 1-0.

As it stood, United were two points ahead of their rivals but a winning goal would see Mancini's Manchester City overtake them courtesy of goal difference. In the ninety-fourth minute at approximately 5.50p.m Sergio Aguero became the difference between Manchester being red and blue. He was the difference between mimicking a certain success in 1999 of their rivals and once again falling short.

The Argentine forward skipped a challenge in the area with only thing coursing through the blue-blooded City fans: shoot! Aguero rifled in a right-footed effort which beat Paddy Kenny and QPR on that day, 3-2. Subsequently, the now-famous cries from *Sky Sports* commentator Martin Tyler capped the conclusion of a thrilling ninety minutes of football. United had to settle for a trophyless season and second place whilst City had built the initial blocks dominating world football.

What if Sergio Aguero's ninety-fourth minute effort was put harmlessly wide and Manchester City drew

2-2 that afternoon to hand Manchester United a twentieth league crown?

Manchester City fans dispersed quickly after the final whistle on the final day of the season, not waiting for the lap of honour which is tradition with English clubs in their final home league match, as in the north-east, Sir Alex Ferguson was waiting to collect his 13th league title with United, and their twentieth overall at the Stadium of Light.

Ferguson labels the season "a poor one" in terms of their European exploits which were pointed towards the UEFA Europa League after Christmas, upon their elimination from the Champions League group stages courtesy of FC Basel in December.

The Manchester United manager still vowed to strengthen the squad in pre-season ready to retain their Premier League and win a 21st league crown, a third in succession.

However, prior to all of the post-season rigmarole of transfer rumours and done deals was the European Championships and Roy Hodgson had a big decision to make in his squad selection for the tournament. Following incidents which took place earlier in the season between John Terry and Rio Ferdinand's brother, Anton, who played for QPR, the two hadn't appeared together for England after the racial arguments which took place in QPR's 1-0 win over nine-man Chelsea in October 2011.

Terry, the former England captain, was replaced as holder of the famous armband after Roy Hodgson's announcement as manager, he appointed Steven Gerrard as the captain with a certain Rio Ferdinand as vice-captain for the tournament at the press conference which announced his squad selections.

Hodgson claimed that whichever decision he made, there would have been a rift in the camp and he felt that because Rio was coming off the high of winning another league title with Manchester United, his sixth since joining the club in 2003, he should be selected ahead of John Terry.

Terry was in court following the tournament and days before the squad selection he had to watch his side in the UEFA Champions League final against Bayern Munich, where they were without their suspended captain and went down 2-1 after extra time thanks to a penalty from Thomas Muller who scored both goals in what became Didier Drogba's final moments in a Chelsea shirt.

Hodgson stated that he risked the Chelsea contingent emulating the upheaval in the French camp in the FIFA World Cup two years previously and he immediately set to work as the England manager, picking up two pre-tournament friendly victories over Belgium and Norway with ease.

After the group stages, Hodgson's decision of plumping for Ferdinand over Terry was being labelled as a "shrewd one" by the nation's sports journalists as the United defender even scored in the final group match against Ukraine in the 3-1 win. England qualified for a quarter final against Italy with seven points amassed in the groups, beating Sweden on the way 2-1 as well as being held by France in a timid goalless encounter. France would later be eliminated in the last eight by Spain.

England, though, wouldn't share the similarities with the French as they soldiered through a quarter final barrage by the Italians and reached the dreaded penalty shootout, where the fate of five of their last previous nine major tournaments ended in a loss. Their record of penalty shootout reads as such, one win over Spain in the European Championships in 1996 before losses at the semi-final stage in the 1990 World Cup and Euro 96 to Germany and a second round shootout defeat to Argentina in the 1998 FIFA World Cup.

This trend continued at the turn of the century with successive quarter final shootout defeats to the Portuguese in the 2004 European Championships and subsequent 2006 FIFA World Cup tournament.

This tournament would be subvert the conventions as Ashley Cole stepped up and converted the crucial penalty in Kiev, beating Italy 5-4 in the shootout which left Germany—the usual stumbling block in the past two semi-final occasions in which England reached that stage at a major tournament.

Two goals from Wayne Rooney finally regained the United forward's scoring touch after suspension which ruled him out of the opening two matches as England surged beyond Germany in a slender 2-1 victory for Hodgson's side. This left the World and European Champions in Spain in the final as their opponents.

The English media were in buoyant mood despite the nature of their opponents for the Sunday final in Kiev and betting prices were short on England winning their first European Championship in Ukraine, over the pre-tournament favourites and two-time champions—Spain.

The balloon filled with the patriotic and optimistic dreams of a nation was well and truly popped in the face of the English after they collapsed due to a sumptuous display from Spain in the final. Hodgson's men lost out 3-1 in their first major tournament final since 1966, but the England side were still deemed heroes upon their return to the country.

The tournament left a few overhanging questions about the future of Robin van Persie after the previous season's Premier League top goalscorer dried up in the tournament. The Dutchman scored once in a dismal campaign for the Netherlands as they were eliminated after three losses to Denmark, Portugal and Germany in the group stages.

Undeterred by this, Roberto Mancini delivered a crucial phone call to Arsene Wenger of Arsenal following the championships, declaring his interest in the Dutch forward. A week or so later and the 27 million pound deal was sealed and announced as well as, according to a majority of Manchester City fans, the league title according to a lot of who were raving about their marquee summer signing.

Across the city, meanwhile, Ferguson could only rely on the duo of Shinji Kagawa and Alex Buttner as his only signings for the summer in a window of slim pickings for the United manager. Shinji Kagawa scored a double along with the in-form Wayne Rooney still high off his performances at the European Championships as Everton were sunk 3-0 away at home on the opening weekend of the season.

Van Persie didn't make his City debut until the start of September, by which time, Mancini's side had already dropped four points from two games. Up next, however, were the Dutchman's former club in Arsenal at his prior stomping ground, the Emirates Stadium.

Two goals from the Dutchman and a chorus of boos later had revitalised Mancini and City as they soon clambered above Manchester United into their top spot with a 2-0 win at home to their fierce rivals, Van

Persie scoring both to take his Premier League tally to thirteen after just ten matches in the blue of City in November at the Etihad Stadium.

Ferguson was rueing his missed opportunities in the off-season as his summer signings in Shinji Kagawa was sidelined for the rest of the season with a broken ankle whilst Buttner wasn't deemed ready for the first team yet. Meanwhile, on a weekend where United were humbled by Norwich City at home, losing 2-0 at Old Trafford, Van Persie drew all the plaudits as he opened up the gap at the top of the league to seven points in January with all four goals in a 4-2 win over Aston Villa. City looked to be cruising to a first Premier League title.

Just two days later, Roberto Mancini held an emergency press conference to announce the most ground-breaking transfer in the sport's history. He welcomed Barcelona's Lionel Messi who was fresh off scoring ninety-one goals in the previous calendar year and having recently captured his fourth Ballon d'Or award for being the best footballer in the world.

Messi signed a six-year contract worth well over a hundred million to ply his trade for Manchester City, alongside the likes of Aguero and Van Persie up front after Carlos Tevez departed for Boca Juniors earlier in the month.

The dream team had just plucked their dream player in the world from his comfort zone and snapped up the deal of the millennium for 159 million pounds, breaking the previous world record of the eighty million paid by Real Madrid for Cristiano Ronaldo in 2009.

The upcoming opponents in QPR were victims of the sport's best strike force in the upcoming Premier

League contest as Messi and Van Persie scored seven between them with the former sealing his fifth late on in a commanding 11-0 win at the Etihad Stadium. This eclipsed United's record of a winning-margin in the league which had stood since their 9-0 win over Ipswich Town eighteen years ago. The match also equalled the most goals in a game record in the division, which had stood for almost six years after Portsmouth and Reading battled out a 7-4 scoreline at Fratton Park in September 2007.

Now trailing City by eight points, Ferguson and Manchester United looked outperformed. Two successive losses to Chelsea eliminated them from both the FA Cup fourth round and the League Cup semi-finals as the hunt for an unprecedented quadruple in English football was dwindling by each passing day.

After one of the worst weeks in Manchester United's history, the supporters saw Wayne Rooney stretchered off in a home loss against Arsenal to add salt into the wounds. Across the country, a Lionel Messi-inspired 2-1 win on a cold night at the Britannia Stadium helped widen the gap to double figures—eleven points.

City had got back on track in Europe as well, with the combination of Malaga and Galatasaray surrendering to Lionel Messi in the Champions League knockout stages who had eclipsed the form of Van Persie who became the architect for most of the Argentine's goals.

Four more goals in a Champions League tie away at Real Madrid told the following morning's back pages for itself as City effectively entered themselves into their first Champions League final as they led Real Madrid going into the home second leg, 4-1.

The league was wrapped up a mere three days later as a solitary goal for Robin van Persie secured a 1-0 win over Aston Villa as City strolled to their first Premier League crown, with a Treble looming large on the horizon.

After defeating Chelsea with consummate ease in the Wembley semi-final, they netted one more in the final against Wigan, Messi and Aguero this time combining to score their second FA Cup triumph in three years with a 4-1 win over Wigan.

Just like Manchester United had done fourteen years previously, City were entering unchartered territory — the chance to win the Treble against Bayern Munich, but this time the match would be played out at Wembley Stadium.

Being one of the most successful teams at the new national stadium, City's form at the ground was seemingly reaching a crescendo as two strikes from Lionel Messi yet again set Manchester City on their way for their first ever European accolade.

The city of Manchester was definitely blue now.

20

The New Galacitco

L uis Suarez committed a crime akin to Diego Maradona's exploits in the 1986 FIFA World Cup against England in the same stage in the same tournament twenty-four years later in South Africa when he played in the surprising last eight tie for Uruguay against African hopefuls Ghana.

Uruguay were proving to be one of the tournament's dark horses with the firepower that they possessed through the trio of Diego Forlan, Edinson Cavani and Luis Suarez. The trinity up front for Uruguay netted nine goals between them as Forlan clinched the Golden Ball award for the best player in the tournament and was joint top scorer alongside Thomas Muller, David Villa and Wesley Sneijder.

Uruguay reached the last four, surprising everybody in the tournament in surpassing South American powerhouses Argentina and Brazil to remain the final team from the continent in the final four.

Suarez almost single-handedly sunk South Korea in the last sixteen as two of his three goals in the tournament came in the tense affair which followed an impressive group stage showing where they and Mexico progressed against an imploded French side and underachieving host in the shape of South Africa.

After scoring the winning goal against Mexico, Suarez sealed Uruguay's first place in the group stage which allowed for a much safer passage to the latter stages of the knockout rounds.

After squeezing past the 2002 semi-finalists in South Korea, Uruguay would forge a path through Ghana to their own semi-final, their first appearance in the final four for forty years in what could've prevailed as their third World Cup title, a first in sixty.

The quarter-final tie against Ghana had a lot resting on it and became the most dramatic game in the entire tournament. Ghana were looking to become the first African nation to make the semi-finals of a FIFA World Cup tournament and were flying the flag for the entire continent at the first African-hosted tournament alone.

Sulley Ali Muntari, formerly of Portsmouth, traded a goal with Diego Forlan in normal time before the match reached the final ebb and flow of extra time inside the Soccer City stadium in Johannesburg.

In the thirtieth and final minute of extra time, Ghanian Dominic Adiyiah directed a header past the grounded Uruguayan goalkeeper, Fernando Muslera, but the goal was only impeded by a certain Luis Suarez who palmed the ball clear at the second time of asking. Nonetheless, the Uruguayan and Ajax talisman received his marching orders from the referee and Asamoah Gyan had the chance to make himself a continental hero from the spot.

Pictures could be seen in the tunnel of Luis Suarez waiting with baited breath before celebrating like he had won the tournament when Gyan's spot kick cannoned out of play off the top of the crossbar. Suarez wheeled away in jubilation as Uruguay were given the reprieve of a penalty shootout.

Both Adiyiah and captain John Mensah both had their kicks saved as Sebastian Abreu calmly lofted the ball into the net to claim a final four berth for Uruguay and reclaimed Luis Suarez's dream to play in a FIFA

World Cup final.

Asamoah Gyan labelled Suarez "a hero in his own country" because of blocking the incident which would have surely sealed a semi-final match against the Netherlands for Ghana. Alternatively, Uruguay whimpered out to a 3-2 loss in the next match and would, subsequent to another defeat against Germany in the play-off, come fourth overall in the tournament.

Suarez claimed a contract at Liverpool in January 2011 for a fee being paid to Ajax of 22.8 million as he forged the frontline at Anfield. He guided Liverpool to three successive finishes in the top eight in the Premier League as well as the League Cup in 2012.

Controversy followed him from the FIFA World Cup to Anfield as he has been charged with two offences of biting an opponent both in the Dutch league and in the Premier League. At the time of writing he is currently midway through a ten-match ban for biting Chelsea defender, Branislav Ivanovic.

The back pages have been filled with Suarez-related content, for example, in October 2011 he was charged with a racial incident on Manchester United's Patrice Evra and was consequently banned for eight matches. He has been consistently accused of diving by various managers such as Tony Pulis and David Moyes in the English Premier League as well as being labelled a "disgrace" by retired Manchester United manager Sir Alex Ferguson.

What if Luis Suarez didn't handle the ball on the line in the FIFA World Cup quarter-final in 2010 and Ghana progressed to the semi-finals to face Holland?

The ball evaded the Uruguayan forward as Ghana completed the passage into the semi-finals with a dramatic late 2-1 win in the second half of extra time in the quarter finals in Johannesburg. Aptly, Ghana became the first African nation to reach the final four stage at the first FIFA World Cup to be hosted on African soil.

Asamoah Gyan would break a sturdy Dutch resolve early on in the semi-final encounter but the collective groan of a nation and the entire continent could be faintly heard as a Wesley Sneijder-inspired turnaround helped Holland to their third World Cup final whilst Ghana would ultimately finish fourth at the tournament after losing to Germany in the third-place play-off. Holland would win the tournament thanks to a Nigel de Jong goal in extra time in the 1-0 win over the Spanish whilst Uruguay and Luis Suarez returned to South America after a pleasing tournament.

Suarez had gained some plaudits for his performances at the World Cup, however, and just mere weeks later, the Uruguayan talisman was signed by Real Madrid for 25 million to bolster their attacking options which featured newly signed Mesut Ozil as well as Cristiano Ronaldo, Angel di Maria, Gonzalo Higuain and Karim Benzema.

Jose Mourinho briefly revolutionised the 4-1-2-3 formation as the trio of Ronaldo, Suarez and Benzema led the high risk, high reward tactic at the Bernabeu in the 2010-11 season where the Uruguayan began the season with twenty-four goals in nineteen matches which left Real Madrid aplomb at the top of La Liga in January. As a side they both led the goalscoring charts and amongst the top fourteen of the division, they also conceded the most.

Many journalists were praising the new tactic from a newly adventurous Mourinho. However, Luis Suarez's knee ligament injury would keep him out for three of the final four months in the season which eroded Real Madrid's lead at the top of La Liga from eleven points to mere goal difference.

During Suarez's absence, Real surrendered to a Barcelona masterpiece in the Champions League semi-finals whilst they were defeated by Sevilla in the Copa del Rey quarter finals. The El Clasico was a composed contest which ended 1-1 after Ozil and Messi traded goals inside the Nou Camp.

Barcelona and Pep Guardiola were still knocking on the Madrid door for the La Liga title as Atletico shared the lead at the top with their fierce rivals going into the final three contests. Enter Suarez.

A couple of goals on his return away at Valencia in a 4-2 win allowed them to open up a void of two points from Atletico and Barcelona with a couple of games, which fed the Spanish population an all-important Madrid derby which could have changed the entire face of the league season.

A hat-trick from Ronaldo, of which Suarez assisted twice along with one of Suarez's own meant successive games in which they netted four goals in another commanding victory. The 4-0 win meant Barcelona would leapfrog Atletico but the draw meant that the gap in goal difference seemed unassailable going into the final match.

The routine 2-1 win over Levante would be enough for Real Madrid as Barcelona achieved second place with a 2-2 draw over Getafe. All in all, it was a successful year for Suarez.

A chasm of a year birthed doubts about Luis Suarez at a supposedly "failing" Real Madrid as they sauntered to the La Liga title in the 2011-12 season but would be knocked out in the Copa del Rey and UEFA

Champions League semi-finals, both by Barcelona as they achieved a double-winning season but languished again in second domestically.

Mourinho, Suarez, Ronaldo and co. had pipped Guardiola and Messi's Barcelona to successive league titles but pressure was grinding down on Mourinho, as he seemed pressured into changing his tactics for European fixtures.

In the summer of 2012, both Manchester City and Barcelona jostled for the signature of Luis Suarez but the Uruguayan pledged his future to the Galacticos by signing a five-year contract at the Bernabeu worth up to 57 million. Adding to this lucrative contract, Mario Balotelli joined with the pair of Benzema and Higuain distributed to the Premier League clubs in Manchester City and Arsenal respectively.

The pressure arising throughout the summer had seemingly vanished due to the dealings from Mourinho in the summer but a pre-season training session in Los Angeles would soon all change that.

A two-footed challenge from the newly-signed 'Super Mario' Balotelli on Luis Suarez initiated a brawl which saw Suarez suspended by the club for "use of foul language" which took place and overshadowed the pre-season for Real Madrid.

After four matches out through the club's self-imposed suspension, the Uruguayan is benched for the opening 2012-13 La Liga contest away at Atletico Madrid where Mario Balotelli achieved all of the accolades, scoring twice in a 3-1 win.

When being substituted for Luis Suarez, neither party acknowledged any form of greeting or handshake as Suarez played out a flat latter fifteen minutes in a crucial league match for which he received criticism whilst Balotelli remained golden in the eyes of the Spanish media.

Balotelli was an integral part of the Italian European Championship winning squad during the summer and was rated highly after scoring four times in the tournament which included the final's solitary goal where Italy defeated Spain 1-0. Following the tournament, Super Mario was highly sought after throughout Europe for which Real were first to the punch in terms of receiving his signature for a 34 million pound signing from Manchester City in the later ebbs of the transfer window.

After the opening day defeat, Suarez doesn't feature from the substitutes bench and Jose Callejon is preferred as a substitute in the following three matches, including the Champions League opener against Juventus where Balotelli and Ronaldo both netted in a crucial 2-1 win in Turin in the group stages.

Spanish media outlet, Marca, reported that after his unused substitute appearance in Turin that Suarez hadn't returned to Madrid with the rest of the team but instead flew out to Uruguayan capital Montevideo, instead.

There was apparently no contact made from either party going into the next La Liga match where a Mario Balotelli hat-trick sunk Osasuna 3-0 at the Bernabeu. If the Uruguayan's future was in doubt during the summer, these inklings were reaching fever pitch from the Real supporters.

In an October interview with Marca, Suarez stated that he wished to stay in South America and had already handed in a transfer request which was vehemently declined by both Jose Mourinho and club president, Perez. This interview followed a damning display from Real and Balotelli as the Italian striker was sent off in a 4-0 thrashing away at Barcelona in the Nou Camp as Messi and Barca leapfrogged Real in both the La Liga standings and in the goalscoring charts.

Real were third in the table behind Valencia as well as Barcelona by the time Luis Suarez returned to the starting line-up in March 2013. Four points was the deficit and aptly enough, Mourinho announced Suarez in the line-up for the return fixture at the Bernabeu against Barcelona.

Real were clinging onto a place in both the Copa del Rey and Champions League second legs and also in the title race. Mourinho was desperate for the club's fallen hero to drag them out of the rut the squad were in as his place at the famous club was becoming increasingly precarious.

For the first time since Balotelli's signing in July 2012, Suarez partnered the Italian up front as four goals between the pair had both beaten Barcelona 5-2 and reduced the deficit back to a point as well as consolidating the relationship between Suarez and Balotelli.

With Suarez back in the fold, Real regain their places in the final four of both the Copa del Rey and the Champions League with wins over Getafe and Arsenal respectively in April.

The Uruguayan netted 17 times in the final fourteen matches of the season as Real closed in on an unprecedented treble. The first contest was the cup final against Real Sociedad where Suarez netted the only goal in the final which had Real on the first rung on the ladder to football immortality.

A 7-1 win from Barcelona over Deportivo meant Real

Madrid had to beat Sevilla on the final day to be sure of a third successive league title under Mourinho's tenure at the club. With the game poised at 2-2, Angel di Maria was tripped in the penalty area in the 73rd minute. Luis Suarez rushed to pick the ball up to seemingly convert the league title-winning penalty before Mario Balotelli physically pushed the Uruguayan over in the box to retrieve the ball.

After the small scuffle, Suarez lunged at Mario Balotelli, forcing them both and the referee onto the ground. Five minutes passed before the majority of the twenty other players and the assistant referees broke the pair up. In an instant, Real had gone from a title-winning penalty to being sent down to nine men with seventeen minutes remaining.

Cristiano Ronaldo converted the penalty but a late Sevilla onslaught ushered in a sixth goal in the game as Real tied 3-3 in Seville, the actions of two egos effectively handing Barcelona a first league title since 2010.

A week had passed before Real Madrid decided to fine both Luis Suarez and Mario Balotelli 100,000 euros on the eve of the UEFA Champions League with Barcelona at Wembley in the second all-Spanish final in 2013.

The teamsheets saw both Luis Suarez and Mario Balotelli starting up front for Real from the outset with Barcelona chasing a league and Europe double, Real were simply reduced to a cup double after the Copa del Rey triumph earlier in May.

Just thirty minutes later, journalists and the world's media inside the stadium were handed fresh teamsheet which saw Jose Callejon and Sami Khedira in the squads in place of the two forwards, without the tumultuous pairing of Suarez and Balotelli even amongst the substitutes.

The scenes inside the ITV studio in Wembley were akin to the Ronaldo FIFA World Cup final teamsheet fiasco in 1998. Two hours later, Adrian Chiles and the group were left to mull over a simple 5-1 win for Barcelona over Real Madrid in Mourinho's most embarrassing evening as a manager.

Real announced the sales of both Luis Suarez and Mario Balotelli to Chelsea and Juventus respectively before sacking Jose Mourinho a day later whilst the events leading up to the final remained a mystery to everyone.

In July, a void of six weeks later, *Sky Sports* broke the news that another scuffle broke out in the dressing room between Luis Suarez and Mario Balotelli as the two divided the entire dressing room with both Angel di Maria and Cristiano Ronaldo vouching for Suarez and the likes of Iker Casillas, Sergio Ramos and Pepe siding with the Italian as Real lunged themselves into disrepute.

Barcelona would win the next four La Liga titles whilst Real Madrid slipped as low as fourth in La Liga with successive quarter final eliminations in the Champions League in the forthcoming years. Mourinho brought a couple of league titles before his time was up in 2017 at Stamford Bridge whilst he coached Luis Suarez as his new signing to just seven matches after he was sent off three times in those paltry matches which garnered just one goal before being sold onto Cruzeiro.

Balotelli had a successful career at Juventus, finishing third in the 2016 Ballon d'Or and winning a successive European Championship with Italy whilst winning four Serie A titles and a Europa League crown and even reaching the 2018 UEFA Champions League final, where they were defeated by Manchester United.

21

Ronald'oh!

At the 1998 FIFA World Cup, Ronaldo was enjoying the peak of his footballing career. He was playing his club football at the Italian club, Inter Milan whilst also becoming one of the first names on the Brazilian national side's teamsheet. He appeared in every group game at the tournament in France, scoring once as Brazil ran through a group containing Norway, Morocco and Scotland.

Two goals in a knockout stage match against Chile in a 4-1 demolition of the fellow South American nation as well as a crucial opener against the Dutch in a semi-final saw the Brazilian birthed onto the world football scene—the hosts France awaited the world champions in the final, who were looking for their first ever World Cup accolade whilst Brazil were the defending champions and on the hunt for their fifth, a tournament record.

Although the likes of Davor Suker, Gabriel Batistuta and Christian Vieri had outscored the Brazilian, big things were expected of Ronaldo approaching the final at the Stade de France on the 12th of July, 1998.

However, Des Lynam of the BBC along with John Motson, Jimmy Hill, David Ginola and Gary Lineker were involved in a television investigation half an hour before the final in Paris in the channel's build up to the most important match in world football.

That investigation was because of Brazil's failure to warm up on the pitch prior to the match as well as leaving out their star player, their centrepiece in Ronaldo off the teamsheet.

This stunned the viewing public as well as the journalists crammed into the 80,000-seater stadium who were handed the sheets. Just minutes from kick-off, the journalists were informed of a change in the teamsheets as Ronaldo was re-instated back into the line-up for the final in Paris.

Brazil floundered to a 3-0 victory as the French outclassed an under-par Brazil and Ronaldo who were obviously off-colour and completely dismantled following the day's events.

What if Ronaldo missed the 1998 FIFA World Cup final after his seizure on the morning of the final in Paris?

Rumblings were emanating from the Brazil camp hours from the final against the hosts, France that their star player and forward who had netted four times in the tournament would be left out due to a "serious medical emergency" of which the details would become clearer after the final.

France won the final 3-1 thanks to a double from Zinedine Zidane which cancelled out Bebeto's opener in the early stages of the match. The Brazil side were visibly dejected throughout the contest which was effectively finished after Emmanuel Petit's late goal for France. Pundits predicted that Brazil would have won the match with Ronaldo despite what was announced as a seizure the following morning.

The entirety of the footballing media converged on the idea that with a fresh Brazilian side and a fully fit Ronaldo, they would have won their fifth FIFA World Cup in Paris on that July evening.

After a season at Inter Milan, Ronaldo agreed

termination of his contract at the Italian club and returned to the sport after a fifteen month absence in October 1999 in a post-season friendly with Cruzeiro's first team against Bayern Munich.

Averaging at over a goal a game in his season and a half back in his native Brazil, Liverpool landed Ronaldo in July 2001 for a fee of £21 million for the seemingly rejuvenated Brazilian forward who hadn't proven himself on the big stage since the World Cup three years ago. He had only earned two international appearances, scoring a hat-trick in the second against Colombia a month before his switch to Merseyside.

The hiatus from the burning spotlight of mainstream football didn't take its toll on Ronaldo as proven in his first few competitive appearances for Liverpool, as he scored twice in the Charity Shield against Manchester United in the 3-1 victory before scoring in matches against Bolton Wanderers in the Premier League and Bayern Munich in the UEGA Super Cup triumph in late August.

Although Liverpool didn't surpass their haul of three cup trophies, the combination of Michael Owen and Ronaldo almost unlocked the portion of the Liverpool trophy cabinet which housed the Premier League titles which had been gathering dust for quite some time.

A double in the FA Cup final sealed successive domestic cup crowns in a 5-1 mauling of Manchester City in the final before losing out on the craved top flight title to Arsenal by a point. A run in the UEFA Champions Oeague in which they were eliminated by Real Madrid in the semi-finals was a club record after the Heysel Stadium disaster in 1985.

Four goals from as many international appearances at the start of the 2001-02 season in the South American qualifying zone sealed Brazil's passage into yet another World Cup which, for the first time, was being held in Asia. This featured a brace in October over Peru which completed a late turnaround with goals in the final fifteen minutes and in turn officially booked them a seat the on the 32-team plane to South Korea and Japan.

This tournament would be the highlight of Ronaldo's career.

Ronaldo's place wasn't sealed after the emergence of Ronaldinho and the form of Rivaldo in the previous season. However, thanks to an injury to the latter, Ronaldo was granted a starting eleven berth for the opening match against Turkey by manager, Luiz Felipe Scolari.

The speculation dumbfounded many supporters of the national side who four years previously were lauding the efforts of the forward. On his first season back in Europe, Ronaldo netted forty-two times in fifty appearances and was a front runner for the 2002 European footballer of the year award. To grant access once more into that prestigious club, Ronaldo would have to shine at the World Cup tournament.

If the first twenty minutes were to go by, plaudits and accolades were almost definitely forthcoming for Brazil and Ronaldo. Three goals in the opening quarter of the match for Liverpool's number ten set him and Brazil on their way for a formidable victory over Turkey. A Hasan Sas goal for Turkey was sandwiched in between another two goals for Ronaldo as he matched the record of Oleg Salenko's five goals in a World Cup match when he scored five goals in Russia's 6-1 triumph over Cameroon at the 1994 World Cup tournament in the United States.

In some tournaments, that goal alone could land the Golden Boot at the doorstep of the goalscorer. However, Ronaldo wasn't done by a long shot in terms of goals.

Two more goals helped Brazil in a 4-0 win over China in their second match which effectively qualified them for the knockout stage with a match to spare. Ronaldo was just three goals off Gerd Muller's long-standing record for FIFA World Cup goals, scoring eleven from the three tournaments he had participated in. However, after being unused in the 1994 tournament and only playing twice in the 2002 tournament, there was many within the media who predicted he would equal the record before the end of the tournament--if not group stage.

Costa Rica were still vying to join Brazil in the last sixteen but the Samba nation stood in their way of a berth in the knockout stages. A goal from Paulo Wanchope had Brazil panicked going into the final twenty minutes of the match. Turkey soon turned around their fortunes due to a winner in their final group match against China and a turnaround from Ronaldinho and Ronaldo which mirrored the win against Peru in qualification.

Ronaldo was up to eight goals and was sauntering to the Golden Boot award with only Miroslav Klose in remote contention despite a void of four goals to make up following a rich vein form for Germany in the group stages, they were becoming the second favourites to lift the Jules Rimet trophy after the eliminations of France and Argentina.

A training session the morning prior to the second round clash against Belgium could have been the difference between a humiliating exit from the tournament and a fifth notch of Brazil's World Cup bedpost. A late tackle from Cafu on Ronaldo seemingly signalled the end of the forward's tournament in a well documented training session as Belgium were expected to roll over for the four-time champions in Kobe, Japan.

Many in the media jumped the gun before the official teamsheet news an hour before kick off the following morning. The 2002 second round match was mirroring the final in terms of Ronaldo's participation. A suspected broken metatarsal bone was being thrown around miraculously in sports newsrooms, the bone had become trendy and infamous after English duo Gary Neville and David Beckham broke the same bone in the build-up to the tournament.

Gary Lineker was able to report, prior to the kick-off, that Ronaldo was in fact on the team sheet and he would score the winning goal in a surprisingly tight 2-1 affair, scoring his ninth goal of the tournament which meant England were approaching on the Brazil horizon in the quarter final.

The aforementioned David Beckham had missed out on a place in Sven-Goran Eriksson's England squad for the tournament due to his broken foot which many thought he was capable of recovering. Without his leadership, England grazed themselves through their second round encounter against Denmark, winning 1-0 thanks to Ronaldo's Liverpool teammate, Michael Owen.

The club mates would be sparring in the quarter final but it would be neither men on the scoresheet as a ludicrous Ronaldinho free-kick allowed celebration in a 1-0 win and yet another semi final appearance where a reunion with Turkey was on the cards.

Two goals from Ronaldo were enough for the forward to level Muller's record for goals at FIFA World Cup t fourteen strikes in a training exercise for the South Americans, winning 4-1 in the semi-final where the void of quality was very evident. Ronaldo could surpass Gerd Muller's scoring record at the tournament in the final against Germany who had steamrolled through USA and co-hosts South Korea in previous rounds.

Oliver Kahn in the German net was keeping the leading Brazilian lights at bay for the majority of the contest whilst Ronaldo's nearest contender for the golden boot award, Miroslav Klose was having similar fortunes in front of goal, putting all five of his first half efforts off target.

The stalemate would be prized apart by none other than Ronaldo who would net his fifteenth FIFA World Cup goal, beating Muller's record as Brazil claimed their fifth title with a slender 1-0 triumph over a defensively solid German outfit.

After his eleven goals at the World Cup, Ronaldo became the most sought after asset in the whole of world football but Liverpool somehow managed to escaped the transfer market unscathed and their forward, Ronaldo untouched.

A Premier League title was still out of reach for the Merseysiders in May 2003, as Manchester United beat them 3-1 at Old Trafford on the penultimate day of the season to reclaim the Premier League crown. The following season would be completely different.

Thirty wins from the season and a record-equalling thirty-four goals in a Premier League season for Ronaldo meant that Liverpool could celebrate a 19th league crown thanks to the quarters of Carragher,

Owen, Ronaldo and Gerrard who remained a solid cornerstone throughout the 2003-04 season where a UEFA Champions League final appearance was made for Liverpool, a first in 19 years.

Unfortunately, a 1-0 win over Juventus from 1985 couldn't be repeated as Liverpool's Ronaldo misfired in the final before losing on penalties to a Juventus side which were expected to roll over for the English side. The difference between winning and losing in the 2004 UEFA Champions League final for Liverpool meant the sale of their prized asset, Ronaldo as he soon switched to Barcelona, joining up with Ronaldinho for €52 million.

Whilst the sale of Ronaldo might have spelled the doom for Liverpool, it funded the purchases of Thierry Henry and Frank Lampard which in turn resulted in the successful UEFA Champions League run of 2004-05 when a simple 3-1 win over AC Milan in Istanbul coupled with a successive triumph in the Premier League had Liverpool onto 20 league titles and wondering "Ronaldo who?!"

The Brazilian forward would only play four more years in Europe, retiring back to Brazil in 2008 but would only claim two La Liga titles as Real Madrid remained largely more successful in Europe, winning the Champions League in 2006 and 2008.

Ronaldo was in the company of Pele and Romario to score over a thousand goals in his career after five more illustrious years at Cruzeiro in which he received a runners-up medal at the 2011 FIFA Club World Cup tournament, losing out to his former club in Liverpool.

22

Michael 'Sicknote' Owen

At the 1998 FIFA World Cup, Michael Owen exploded onto the world footballing scene with his spectacular, almost mirror-image goal of Diego Maradona against Argentina. His previous exploits for Liverpool had warranted a place in Glenn Hoddle's England squad for the 18-year old which included scoring on his professional debut against Wimbledon in the Premier League in May 1997 before sharing the divisional Golden Boot the following season prior to the tournament.

The goal of the tournament for the 1998 World Cup was all in vain as England exited in the same second round match, losing to Argentina via a missed David Batty penalty in a shootout. Owen's stock was only on the rise after two goals in his first international tournament after retaining his Premier League golden boot trophy in the 1998-99 season alongside Dwight Yorke and Jimmy Floyd Hasselbaink.

A regular place was being earned in the national side for the Liverpool forward and it seemed that Owen was the man to finally break the long-standing goalscoring record held by Sir Bobby Charlton. Goals were always in the Liverpool attacker but success wasn't bred with Owen's goalscoring record as Liverpool were constantly drifting above and below the line which separated glory in the UEFA Cup and the UEFA Champions League.

However, after the abysmal display at the European

Championships in 2000 following a group stage elimination, success followed at a club level. Liverpool breached the top three in the Premier League to grant them access in Europe's top club competition in a season where Owen amassed 16 league goals in the 2000-01 season. The silverware appeared in the trophy cabinet in the latter part of the season for Liverpool, the League Cup was wrapped up with a penalty shootout win over second-tier club Birmingham City at the Millennium Stadium.

Three months later, Liverpool returned to the Welsh capital to claim more glory. However, in between the two dates in Cardiff a second trophy was won - a first Liverpool title in Europe since 1985. This time, the UEFA Cup was claimed in an enthralling 5-4 win over Spanish club Alaves in extra time, in the competition's greatest final. Michael Owen will always be remembered for that particular season in turning around the FA Cup final on its head against Arsenal in the final minutes.

Arsenal had taken a relatively late lead in the 72nd minute through Freddie Ljungberg but it would be Liverpool celebrating in Cardiff after two goals from the later-announced European footballer of the year for 2001 in Michael Owen. The 83rd and 88th minute strikes from the English international meant a sixth FA Cup for Liverpool but except for a Charity Shield accolade later that year and a 2003 League Cup win in which Owen figured in and scored against Manchester United would be the only club honours earned by Owen before his switch to Real Madrid in 2004.

He remains, at the time of writing, the player to have scored the most goals per minute in La Liga as he was often used as a substitute in his one year at the Spanish club. In the time of players such as Cristiano Ronaldo, Lionel Messi and Ronaldinho is a huge achievement for the English forward.

Owen turned out for such clubs as Newcastle United, Manchester United and Stoke City in the English Premier League, finally claiming his sole Premier League crown in 2011 for Manchester United in a league where he contributed 150 goals to the league, ranking 7th on the all-time goalscoring charts at the time of writing behind the likes of former teammates in Robbie Fowler and Alan Shearer.

His career was cut short in May 2013 when he announced his retirement due to the frequency of injuries which blemished his career which was left without an international accolade along with diminished club honours for one of the greatest English strikers in football.

We join Michael Owen's career at the end of the 2001-02 season where a fresh Liverpool forward is hoping to spearhead an England team into the 2002 World Cup. What if Michael Owen's career wasn't hampered by injury?

A 1-1 draw in Japan against Sweden wasn't the ideal way that Owen and England wished to begin the tournament but Argentina were the upcoming opponents and one of the favourites to take the title in the Far East.

Instead of buckling under the strain of soft tackle in the penalty area, the feet of Owen travelled him through five bodies in the Argentine penalty area before slotting the ball into an empty net, replicating his goal from four years previously, but in a more compressed fashion, within the vicinity of the small area.

Ariel Ortega would level an intense match up prior to the half time break but a lacklustre second half performance from the Argentines allowed the Liverpool forward to ghost through on two particular occasions which would warrant goals in a 3-1 victory for the English over Argentina. A draw with Nigeria would seal England's path to the knockout stages but Owen was the English assassin in front of goal, scoring the only goal of the game in a comfortable 1-0 win which left them Turkey in the second round.

Two more against the Turks in a 4-0 drubbing of the European opposition left Senegal between Owen and Brazil in a semi final showdown. Owen was tied with Ronaldo on six goals going into the quarter finals stage but Owen couldn't find the net, as England progressed in a slender 1-0 victory thanks to a David Beckham penalty.

In the match which was effectively billed as a showdown between the two world's greatest forwards in Owen and Ronaldo, the English prevailed 2-1 between the forwards whilst the actual contest finished 3-2 which marked England's second World Cup final.

France, the holders and pre-tournament favourites, were England's opponents in the final in Yokohama. It was a simple war of attrition between the two European nations, neither side were committing players in the opposition penalty area as they were too scared of making mistakes. The game ventured into the later echelons of the extra time period, with one goal gifting either side the World Cup based on the golden goal ruling.

On the 107th minute, a long crossfield ball from Steven Gerrard through on the French goal and with the World Cup trophy in his eyes but before he could stretch for the ball he was clutching at his hamstring. Was his injury-laden spell about to continue?

Four minutes later, Owen was poking home the only goal of the contest after he recovered from his bout of cramp to tuck away a scrappy goal to win England's second World Cup thanks to Owen who notched up his tally to nine.

After the summer of English celebration, many clubs were starting to open up their cheque books for the signature of Owen, with a bid coming in from rivals, Manchester United for 51 million which would have broken the world transfer fee record but Liverpool slapped a release clause of 105 million on the forward which, safe to say, warned United off the scent.

Fast forward a year and a Premier League title later and Liverpool had re-stocked their starting line-up fuelled with the money which a certain release clause allowed them. Owen's thirty goals in the Premier League as well as netting seven in Europe which took Liverpool to a Champions League semi-final encounter where they ultimately lost to Barcelona - Michael Owen's new employer.

The likes of Rivaldo, Ronaldo and Figo - all established figures in Barcelona were soon joined by fellow England international David Beckham following a £25 million purchase from Manchester United. In the 2003-04 season, Barcelona demolished the league with the combination of Owen and Ronaldo which amassed 16 goals between them in the previous summer's World Cup had contributed 73 between them in the La Liga season.

A young Cristiano Ronaldo, after a season of bench warming at Manchester United was snapped up a cut price by the Nou Camp club in preparation for the 2004-05 season. Whilst Owen could claim countless league titles upon his retirement in 2014 at the age of 34 but could only remember 2007 as his stand out year at Barca.

Owen and Beckham were both at Barcelona, coming off the back of a poor World Cup defence. The 2006 FIFA World Cup will be remembered for the crash and burn of the defending champions, England. After adding two more to his tally of eleven World Cup goals in a perfect group stage campaign which saw wins against Sweden, Paraguay and Trinidad & Tobago before being dumped out of the tournament in a second round penalty shootout against Ecuador. Brazil defeated Italy to win their fifth World Cup which inspired the Brazilian contingent inside the Barcelona camp.

Ronaldo netted fifty-three goals in the 2006-07 which had Owen a game against Liverpool which stood in front of a treble-winning season and a term which was a disappointing campaign containing only two trophies. For most clubs that would mark a great season, but as one stand in the Nou Camp reads, Barcelona are "mes que un club" (more than a club).

The jeers rang out around the Liverpool end when Owen's name was announced through the tannoy system and after Steven Gerrard's opening strike on 57 minutes, it looked as though Owen would have to wait a little while long to be holding the Champions League.

On what was pre-announced as Ronaldo's final game in Europe, he climaxed his Barcelona career with an equaliser on the cusp of second half stoppage time which dejected a Liverpool side seemingly destined to collect their sixth European Cup title, a second in three years.

With Gerrard and new signing, Zlatan Ibrahimovic already substituted with the match already won according to Rafael Benitez, he labelled it in a 2017 interview his "biggest mistake in football to date". Michael Owen would break the hearts of the supporters who used to adore him in the 114th minute, scoring yet another crucial extra time winner which had won him the World Cup five years previously netted him a Champions League medal some ten years after his debut for Liverpool.

With no more honours to be had, Owen set his sights on claiming more silverware for the national team and having being named in the squad for the European Championships in 2008, he was a goal away from tying Sor Bobby Charlton's record having tied Gary Lineker's 48 goals in an England shirt in a pre-tournament friendly against Russia.

A 3-0 win was easily acquired against co-hosts in the opener against Austria but Owen was growing weary of eclipsing Charlton's tally. Germany, a team where one of Owen's finest international moments came in September 2001 after scoring a hat trick in Munich, were upcoming opponents in Group B.

An early goal from German talisman, Miroslav Klose set the tone for a miserable evening as Germany walked away with the top place in the group after a 4-1 demolition. However, a late goal from Owen meant his 49th goal came with no real importance which left Poland standing in their way for another appearance in the knockout stages.

The previous tournament, Owen as a member of the world champions, England were stunned by a

Portuguese side who pipped them to a semi final place in a tight 2-1 victory in Lisbon. Portugal were potential opponents again, prior to the clash against Poland in Klagenfurt.

England went behind to the Polish who were fighting for their own place in the quarter finals. However, by the half-time break was sounded by the referee, not only had England fired themselves into a stupendous 4-1 lead but a hat trick courtesy of Barcelona forward, Michael Owen meant his tally was on 52 goals, officially breaking the long-standing record laid down by the Manchester United great, Sir Bobby Charlton.

Poland scored a consolation goal but the 4-2 victory meant Portugal remained in the quarter final for Harry Redknapp's England outfit. Cristiano Ronaldo was labelled as a big threat prior to the contest but his Barcelona teammate, Michael Owen's two second half goals secured a 2-0 victory which went some way to abolishing the disappointment which followed the high expectations birthed by that Owen goal in the 2002 World Cup final.

Whilst Owen would reach the semi-finals, their European Championship dream would end in yet another semi-final defeat to Germany. This didn't end in the fashion in which their group stage match did, but instead harked back to the penalty shootout defeats of the 1990 FIFA World Cup and the 1996 European Championships.

England wouldn't reach the heights of that famous World Cup win whilst Owen was in the ranks with successive semi-final appearances in major tournaments up until Owen's international retirement after Euro 2012. He will always be remembered for his record-breaking 64 goals in the famous Three Lions shirt and for the numerous personal accolades collected in his 16-year professional career.

23

Scary and Becks

In July 1999, David Beckham married Victoria Adams of the girl group, Spice Girls after his most successful season in football in terms of honours won as Manchester United romped home to three trophies that season which culminated in the dramatic UEFA Champions League final against Bayern Munich in May 1999.

In terms of football, Beckham remains one of the biggest recognisable names on the planet even after his retirement. Through his extensive philanthropy work along with ambassadorial roles for Chinese football as well as the London Olympic bid for the 2012 games alongside Lord Sebastian Coe.

The accolades speak for themselves, he has winner's medals for top flight leagues in England (6), United States (2), France and Spain (both 1 title). Loan spells at Preston North End and AC MIlan as well as periods at Old Trafford, Real Madrid, Los Angeles Galaxy and Paris Saint-Germain.

Victoria Beckham became a household name alongside her husband David, even after the break up of the Spice Girls in 2000, and were dubbed 'Posh and Becks' by the tabloids and have an estimated value of £125 million as a couple. As of 2013, the couple have four children, Brooklyn, Romeo, Cruz and Harper and their first-born, Brooklyn, is a part of the Queen's Park Rangers youth squad having played for his father's former employers Los Angeles Galaxy and Paris Saint-

Germain as well as Chelsea earlier in 2013.

It still remains to be seen if Brooklyn can emulate his father's success which brought him the England captaincy as well as an almost record-breaking 115 caps, only bettered by goalkeeper, Peter Shilton. Personal accolades now crowd Beckham's trophy cabinet, and they're largely associated with football, not the Grammy's or MTV VMAs for Victoria.

The governing bodies which occupy that particular cabinet are in the neighbourhood of the PFA, UEFA and FIFA as well as being named in Pele's list of 100 greatest living footballers. Beckham will be immortalised in the world of football and the 'Brand Beckham' is constantly improving in its popularity. However, it could have been different.

We join David Beckham in January 1998, Manchester United are on the verge of another Premier League title ahead of Arsenal. Leicester City are the opponents at Old Trafford on the 31st of January in the Premier League and an appearance by Mel B - Scary Spice of the Spice Girls - boosted Beckham's morale.

Tony Cottee's first half strike was cancelled out by a trademark free kick from none other than Manchester United's new number seven, taking over the jersey from the retired Eric Cantona. A further two goals from Andy Cole helped United to a 3-1 win which helped them to regain a seven point lead at the top of the Premier League.

In the following three matches, Beckham netted four times in the Premier League, including his first professional hat-trick against Bolton Wanderers, opening up an eleven point lead over Arsenal. The next morning, *The Sun* splashed pictures of 'Scary and

Becks' stumbling out of a restaurant where the popster exclaimed that the England winger had proposed to her.

Beckham's form improved further, scoring twice in a crucial match at Old Trafford against second-placed Arsenal and a handful of matches later, the Premier League title was sewn up for a third successive crown in England, Ferguson's fifth in the twelve years he had coached the club.

After coming off stage in Brussels in May 1998 with the Spice Girls, Mel B announced the date for the marriage would be July 17th, 1999. However, on that date, David Beckham was being paraded in front of 50,000 in the streets, wearing a certain famous black and white shirt.

Rolling back down the hill of the proposal and reports were emanating in December 1998 that David Beckham had been spotted stumbling out of nightclubs with Mel B's friend and colleague, Victoria Adams. Beckham was growing restless, his form was deteriorating and after such a promising FIFA World Cup in which he helped England to a quarter final defeat to Holland by scoring in the penalty shootout against Argentina in the second round.

After being benched for several matches after under performing, the glossy magazines were reporting correctly as the speculation of Posh Spice was both breaking the pop group and the world's biggest engagement apart. Subsequently, the marriage was pushed forward to February 1999 and five days later he netted twice in an FA Cup fifth round tie against Fulham.

There was some ground to be made up to catch up to Arsenal in the Premier League title race as with nine matches remaining, five points was the void. The brief upturn in fortunes for both Beckham and Manchester United was crushed almost immediately after elimination in both the FA Cup quarter final against Chelsea and in the UEFA Champions League at the same stage thanks to a Diego Simeone-inspired Inter Milan.

Approaching the crucial away day at Anfield, United needed a win to overtake Arsenal with only a handful of matches remaining in the season reports were simmering about David Beckham's extra-marital business with a certain Victoria Adams, formerly of the Spice Girls and star of a diminishing solo career.

Forty-two minutes was all Beckham could achieve at Anfield as Ferguson hauled him off the pitch in an early substitution which was a consequence Beckham paid for a poor performance in which United ultimately lost 4-1 in a display which effectively left the club without a trophy in the 1998-99 season.

A bust-up between Ferguson and Beckham was the main subject of the back pages and the winger never pulled on the red of Manchester United under his management ever again. Furthermore, divorce was on the cards for Beckham after 3 months of marriage to Mel B after his fling with Posh Spice was made public on a famous May 27th, 1999 publication of *The Sun* which still remains overhanging above the office of NewsCorp's CEO Rupert Murdoch which is now dubbed 'The Discovery of the Century' in a 2023 poll which defeated the discovery of life on Mars in 2018.

The story delivered David Beckham, a one-time shining light in the future of English football, to St. James' Park where he was paraded around as Newcastle United new signing in preparation for the

1999-00 season. He was half of the biggest transfer story in the summer of 1999 as Alan Shearer was the deal breaker for Alex Ferguson as the two players were exchanged in a simple swap.

A year down the road, Beckham was in the squad for the European Championships in Belgium and the Netherlands, re-married to Victoria 'Posh Spice' Beckham and guaranteed UEFA Champions League football after finishing in second place with Newcastle United, behind only Manchester United who had the ammunition of Alan Shearer and Dwight Yorke to fire them to a league and FA Cup double.

Under Keegan, Beckham finally retained his place in the England squad for the first time but after four appearances in the tournament, England were dumped out of the tournament in a quarter final to eventual winners Italy.

Upon the appointment Sven-Goran Eriksson and the retirement of captain Alan Shearer, Beckham was named captain prior to the qualification for the 2002 FIFA World Cup. Beckham and Newcastle would straddle the UEFA Champions League places from 2000 until 2004 upon his transfer to Tottenham Hotspur.

Beckham's finest hour in a Newcastle shirt would come in their now famous 2001-02 UEFA Champions League run. Four goals helped Newcastle overcome two group stages which contained such teams as Real Madrid, Juventus, Bayern Munich and Lyon, winning eight of the twelve matches where they retained an impeccable home record.

St. James' Park became somewhat of a fortress and after three draws and two victories, Newcastle needed a win over Real Madrid which featured the likes of

Ronaldo, Raul and Zidane. After a goal from Guti early on and Roma who were trumping Anderlecht 3-0 by half-time in Brussels, Newcastle were desperate for two goals. Gary Speed netted a goal on 67 minutes before a free-kick four minutes from time from the one and only David Beckham.

Five months later, Beckham was assisting Craig Bellamy in sealing a quarter final place thanks to a 3-1 victory over Lyon which fed them Panathinaikos in the quarter finals. Despite being inexperienced in the tournament, Newcastle were expectant of a victory and a couple of 2-1 triumphs allowed them a European evening at Anfield, another fortress down the years.

The semi-final first leg saw Liverpool hold Beckham's Newcastle to a goalless draw on Tyneside but down in Merseyside, Michael Owen had gifted Liverpool an early lead as they searched for their first European final in almost two decades.

The cauldron of Anfield was tamed in the second half thanks to a goal from youngster, Shola Ameobi which granted Newcastle their first ever European Cup final, based on the away goals rule. Liverpool subsequently crashed out of the title race a couple of weeks later which left the primary clubs of Manchester and Newcastle to jostle for position.

The focus on European dates had sacrificed some of the earlier, more illustrious league form which Newcastle had previewed the rest of the league. However, after a 2-1 home defeat to Derby County, Manchester United claimed the league title the following day in their penultimate match with a win at home to Aston Villa.

One more match would see out a successful Newcastle United season as they travelled the short distance to Hampden Park, Glasgow to face Real Madrid who were in sight of their ninth UEFA Champions League crown whilst Newcastle were looking to decimate their European title virginity.

Beckham outclassed Zidane in the opening stages of the match, unleashing a first half free-kick which beat Iker Casillas all ends up firing Newcastle into the lead going into the half-time break. However, all good things must come to an end but for Newcastle it unfortunately came too prematurely as by the time the final whistle was sounded, two Zinedine Zidane goals coupled with a strike from Raul meant Real Madrid wrapped up another European Cup whilst Beckham was still awaiting a Champions League winner's medal.

Club accolades were never consistently on the horizon of David Beckham's career. He was the nation's hero after the 2002 FIFA World Cup but with a couple of FA Cup crowns with Newcastle in 2004 and Tottenham a year later in his inaugural season at White Hart Lane. League titles that were won in England weren't replicated in his career in Britain but when he was snapped up by AC Milan where he lived out the rest of his career from 2009 to 2013 where he accomplished a treble winning season in 2011-12 in his penultimate season. A couple more Serie A titles alongside a second Coppa Italia crown in 2013 which concluded a solid career, that was always highlighted by the 2002 FIFA World Cup tournament in the Far East.

June 2nd, 2002 marked the first time Beckham led England out in a major tournament as Eriksson helped England defeat his home nation, Sweden thanks to a Sol Campbell header and a strike from Michael Owen.

Two David Beckham free kicks against Argentina would ultimately be the difference between qualification and elimination from the group stages in another 2-0 victory.

A stalemate against Nigeria allowed England through as group winners whilst Argentina crashed and burned out of the tournament. An assist from the number seven helped England trudge through a surprisingly tough Senegalese task in the second round thanks to a golden goal strike courtesy of Steven Gerrard.

Turkey were sent rolling out of the tournament thanks to a double from Emile Heskey as England powered through 6-1 in one of the greatest nights at a FIFA World Cup which would only be bettered by a semi-final date with Brazil four days later where, with the help of a second goal from Beckham and a subsequent penalty, allowed England to dream of a second FIFA World Cup title.

The 3-3 draw was easily the match of the tournament. Brazil surrendered a chance for that fifth World Cup crown thanks to a Ronaldinho missed penalty as England won their first penalty shootout at the third time of asking at a World Cup.

The dream would be crushed on June 30th though. David Beckham wore the heart worthy of the Three Lions which were emblazoned on his chest, as did the other ten English players on the pitch but it wouldn't be enough as Germany won an intense affair, winning 1-0 via a Michael Ballack goal in the second half.

England fans in Yokohama were heartbroken as were the millions watching up and down the country as Germany squeezed through to their fourth World Cup title, levelling with Brazil. David Beckham was branded a national hero, subsequently knighted for his charitable work and services to football in 2018.

A presentation by Club Books
www.club-books.com

UK Ltd.

5B/346/P